Research Report | 2014

Resurgent Resource Nationalism?
A Study into the Global Phenomenon

Research by MISTRA
Edited by Mcebisi Ndletyana and David Maimela

MAPUNGUBWE
INSTITUTE FOR STRATEGIC REFLECTION (MISTRA)

Mapungubwe Institute for Strategic Reflection (MISTRA)
First floor, Cypress Place North
Woodmead Business Park
142 Western Service Road
Woodmead 2191
Johannesburg

First published January 2016

© MISTRA 2016

ISBN 978-1-920655-13-6

REAL AFRICAN PUBLISHERS

Published by Real African Publishers
on behalf of the Mapungubwe Institute for Strategic Reflection
(MISTRA)

PO Box 3317
Houghton
Johannesburg 2041

MAPUNGUBWE INSTITUTE (MISTRA)
[A NON-PROFIT COMPANY][104-474-NPO]
REGISTRATION NUMBER 2010/002262/08
["THE INSTITUTE"]

Printed and bound in South Africa

contents

ACRONYMS

AGIP	Azienda Generale Italiana Petroli (Italian state-owned oil company)
AGOCO	Arab Gulf Oil Company
AIOC	Anglo-Iranian Oil Company
ANP	Agencia Nacional de Petroleo (Brazil)
Aramco	Saudi Arabian Oil Company
AT	Mozambican Tax Authority
BNDES	Banco Nacional de Desenvolvimento Econômico e Social (Brazil Development Bank)
CIL	Coal India Limited
CNPC	China National Petroleum Corporation
COCHILCO	Comisíon Chilena del Cobre (Chile)
CODELCO	Corporación Nacional del Cobre de Chile
Comibol	Corporacion Minera de Bolivia
CVG Minerven	Corporación Venezolana de Guayana Minerven (Venezuela)
CVP	Corporación Venezolana de Petroleós (Venezuela)
CVRD	Companhia Vale do Rio Doce (Brazil)
EIA	Energy Information Administration (US)
ENI	Ente Nazionale Idrocarburi (Italy)
EPSA	Exploration and Production Sharing Agreements
FDI	Foreign Direct Investment
FIPPA	Foreign Investment Promotion and Protection Act (Iran)
GAIL	Gas Authority of India
GATT	General Agreement on Trade and Tariffs
GDP	Gross Domestic Product
GFC	Global Financial Crisis
GNPC	Ghana National Petroleum Corporation
IDH	Impuesto Directo en los Hidrocarburos (Bolivia)
IGAD	Inter-governmental Authority on Development
IMF	International Monetary Fund
IOC	International Oil Company
Lipetco	Libyan Petroleum Company

LNG	Liquefied Natural Gas
MMR	Ministry of Mineral Resources (Mozambique)
MOFNE	Ministry of Finance and National Economy (Sudan)
MOPNG	Ministry of Petroleum and Natural Gas
NBR	National Bureau of Asian Research
NELP	New Exploration Licensing Policy
NIF	National Islamic Front (Sudan)
NIOC	National Iranian Oil Company
NIP	National Petroleum Institute (Mozambique)
NOC	National Oil Company
OAPEC	Organisation of Arab Petroleum Exporting Countries
OBM	Obsolescing Bargaining Model
OGJ	Oil & Gas Journal (US)
OIL	Oil India Limited
ONGC	Oil and Natural Gas Corporation (India)
OSA	Operating Service Agreement
PDVSA	Petroleós de Venezuela
Pemex	Petroleos Mexicanos
Petrobrás	Petroleo Brasileiro (Brazil)
PSCs	Pre-salt Production Sharing Contracts
PSUV	United Socialist Party of Venezuela
SME	Small & Medium Enterprise
SPC	Sudan Petroleum Corporation
SPLM	Sudan People's Liberation Movement
USGS	United States Geological Survey
WB	World Bank
WNPOC	White Nile Petroleum Operating Company
WTO	World Trade Organisation
YPBF	Yacimientos Petroliferos Fiscales de Bolivia
YPF	Yacimientos Petrolíferos Fiscales (Argentina)
YPFB	Yacimientos Petrolíferos Fiscales Bolivanos (Bolivia)
ZCCM	Zambia Consolidated Copper Mines Ltd
ZCI	Zambia Copper Investments Ltd

CHAPTER 1: INTRODUCTION

The period between 2001 and 2008 saw the longest commodities boom in recent history. Resource-rich countries across the world developed more interest in the profits, control and ownership of their natural resources. South Africa, which did not benefit much from the boom in commodity prices, was nonetheless affected by the emergent resource nationalism trend, and it became the focus of the governing party's 2010 National General Council, which ultimately resulted in the constitution of a committee to review the country's policy and legislative framework regarding 'natural wealth beneath the soil'. Although the resurgence of resource nationalism is a recent phenomenon, the idea of state intervention in the economy, and the extractive sector in particular, is not new.

This qualitative study looks at the resurgence of resource nationalism over the past ten years. It discusses the concept of resource nationalism and its manifestation in public policy. It identifies the concerns, drivers and instruments through which resource nationalism is pursued by various mining jurisdictions across regions. It deliberately focuses more on the hydrocarbons sector in order to suit the target audience. The aim is to observe macro-trends emerging in various regions of the world and explore how best private actors can respond to the various forms of resource nationalism.

For the purposes of this study, the focus was to look at resource nationalism as a phenomenon that, at face value, seemed to have coincided with the commodities boom between 2001 and 2008. Although there is reference to economic history, greater emphasis is placed on analysing the previous decade and the central question is: how has the recent wave of resource nationalism manifested itself in public policy within the selected regions and countries?

The report deliberately does not discuss whether state intent in implementing resource nationalism measures mooted expectations. What it does do is discuss the manifestation of resource nationalism and how it affects international oil companies (IOCs).

The report has seven chapters, broken down as follows: Chapter One introduces the report and discusses conceptual and characteristic features of resource nationalism; Chapter Two discusses the African region; Chapter

Three focuses on the Latin American region; Chapter Four deals with the Middle Eastern, Northern and North-Eastern African regions; Chapter Five discusses the European region; Chapter Six focuses on the Asian region, and Chapter Seven concludes with a high-level summary of the major themes explored in the report.

The research team comprised Dr Mcebisi Ndletyana (leader and supervisor), David Maimela, Catherine Kannemeyer and Sedireng Lerakong. This study was conducted for SASOL Ltd.

RESOURCE NATIONALISM AS A GLOBAL PHENOMENON

For many years, natural resources beneath the soil have been accepted as an asset over which states have sovereign rights. This understanding and principle was officially codified in international law as an inalienable right and norm. In 1962, the United Nations took a resolution to declare the 'inalienable right of all states freely to dispose of their natural wealth and resources in accordance with their national interests'.[1]

Poverty, inequality and unemployment characterise most of the resource-rich countries despite their mineral wealth. This, accompanied by the recent sustained commodities boom and the current global financial crisis, have conspired as leading conditions for the emergence of the renewed spate of resource nationalism in these countries.

In order to understand the concept of resource nationalism better, it may be useful to start by defining what it is not. Throughout history, state intervention in the resource sector has taken one of two dominant forms: nationalisation or privatisation. With resource nationalisation, the state has complete ownership of the resources, including control, management, distribution, etc. Privatisation, on the other hand, refers to a process through which the state withdraws ownership either completely, or in part, to allow for private entities or individuals to own the particular resource(s).

The Southern African Institute for Mining and Metallurgy (SAIMM) defines resource nationalism as the combination of people's desire and state action. 'It is the desire of the people of resource-rich countries to derive more economic benefit from their natural resources and the resolution of their governments to concomitantly exercise greater control of the country's natural resource sectors'.[2]

---

1   General Assembly Resolution 1803 (XVII) of 14 December 1962: Permanent sovereignty over natural resources.
2   SAIMM. 2012. 'The Rise of Resource Nationalism: Resurgence of State Control in an Era of Free Markets Or the Legitimate Search for a New Equilibrium? A Study to Inform Multi-stakeholder Dialogue on State-Participation in Mining'.

In other words, resource nationalism relates to property rights and the allocation of the profits that flow from the extraction of resources. Most mineral resources are scarce and finite. These resources are often viewed as occupying a position of strategic importance in countries where they are available and where the state needs to exert control over the necessary feed stocks for the development of the domestic economy. Such interventionist tendencies comprise resource nationalism.

One could argue, depending on epochs and geography, that resource nationalism is conceptualised in many different ways. The concept and application has been contested by academics of various hues and sectional interests of various sorts. However, there is a consensus that the concept refers to the 'extent and type of state intervention' in the extractive sectors of the economy. In most cases, these specifics are defined by the political elite as they are crucial for economic and political purposes. Resource nationalism can be implemented in a number of ways: from state ownership of equity to regulatory control and fiscal benefit. The objectives are either economic or non-economic.

RESOURCE NATIONALISM DRIVERS

In general, the resurgent resource nationalism of the twenty-first century has wider political and social drivers in addition to the traditional economic ones that are usually focused on. These drivers include:

Ideology & politics

Historically, ideology has been a key driver. Expropriation or resource nationalism driven by ideology is relatively predictable because those who build political movements on the back of nationalisation are usually quite transparent in their intentions. Resource nationalism in this context is usually the result of socialist, communist, populist or nationalist ideologies. Political motivations for resource nationalism are far more self-interested – to build popular support and political capital, to placate interest groups (particularly domestic ones) and constituencies, or simply to enrich public officials and/ or political elites. In this case, the state may determine that expropriation may be its most politically expedient option, even if it is not the best long-term solution to successfully developing national resources for the benefit of national development objectives.[3]

---

3   Ian Bremmer and Preston Keat. 2009. *The Fat Tail: The Power of Political Knowledge for Strategic Investing*. Oxford University Press.

Local community demands

Mining companies' visibility in the eyes of local communities is capacious due to the inherent size of mining activities, the impact of these activities on the local environment, as well as on the surrounding communities and the growing understanding by local communities of mining's potential economic benefits. As such, local communities are becoming more perceptive of the value of short-term (majority local) construction (manual employment) created during the development phase of a new project versus longer-term (majority expatriate employees) production and supplier jobs prevalent during the operations phase. Once a mine is built and local jobs dissipate, communities are often left with the impression that miners have not contributed a sustainable local benefit, which can lead to potential community unease, or even unrest, and threaten the mine's social licence to operate. Many mining companies – assuming that the royalties they pay, and the productive relationships they enjoy with the national government – are blindsided by this unexpected reaction at the mine gates. However, in many emerging markets, there is little relationship between national politics and regional realities, especially when a tribal or ethnic divide separates the local populace from those in power in the capital city.[4]

Socio-economic elements

Governments can blame economic problems and the undesirable social conditions of unemployment and poverty on foreign firms and their usurping of national resources. This is particularly relevant when commodity prices are high and foreign mining enterprises are perceived to be achieving super-profits whilst poverty/socio-economic levels remain largely unchanged. Consequently, socio-economic factors, in particular, can create pressure on a state to increase its 'take' from its natural resources. However, states face a difficult dilemma of how to maximise the national benefit from a finite resource while not scaring off investors – in most cases, the state does not have access to the funds or expertise to exploit and develop its natural resources and must rely on foreign investors to do so.[5]

This rationale for resource nationalism usually occurs in countries where one, or a combination of, the following aspects obtain:

* over-dependence on natural resources – lack of economic diversification;
* fast growing populations whose social, educational and health needs are not being satisfied;
* lack of sustainable economic growth;

4   Deloitte & Touche. 'Tracking the trends 2014: The top 10 issues mining companies will face in the coming year'. Available at: http://www.deloitte.com/assets/ [Accessed May 2014].

5   Philip Hill, David Lewis, James Pay, Audley Sheppard and Jo Delaney of Clifford Chance LLP, with PLC Finance. 2012. 'Resource Nationalism: A Return to the Bad Old Days?' Practical Law Company. Available at: www.practicallaw.com [Accessed May 2014].

* jobless growth;
* lack of appropriate infrastructure and social services; and
* pervasive and significant maldistribution of income.

Contractual and Legislative environment

Investment agreements in the extractive industry (mining and oil exploration) usually involve long-term concessions or mining licences that provide for flat royalty and tax rates. These agreements are commonly not well-designed to accommodate significant changes, such as the recent record commodity prices or evolving political, social or economic conditions. These contracts were also agreed upon or negotiated during a time of low market prices when there was less competition and governments were in a weaker position to negotiate. Some contracts are just inherently exploitative, where foreign investors have taken advantage of political instability, corruption or a kleptocratic state to negotiate terms that are often unacceptable by the population or a new government. As a result, host governments often challenge these agreements as unfair, or not sufficiently beneficial to the country.[6] As such, contract reviews can genuinely be linked to a drive for increased transparency and fairness in the mining sector.[7]

Similarly, the legal frameworks governing the minerals industry are frequently outdated or inappropriate and do not maximise the potential benefits government can gain from their resource industry.

RESOURCE NATIONALISM INSTRUMENTS

Nationalisation and Expropriation

Nationalisation is a term used to describe governments asserting control over natural resources by taking privately owned industry or assets into majority (more than 50 percent) government ownership/control. Nationalisation is distinguished from property redistribution in that the government retains control/ownership of nationalised assets. A key issue in nationalisation is payment of compensation to the former owner – the most controversial and extreme nationalisations, known as expropriations, occur when no compensation, or an amount far below the likely market value of the nationalised assets, is paid. Outright expropriation is relatively easy to recognise: the state takes over a business, or nationalises an entire industry, depriving the investors of all benefits associated with ownership and control.

6   Ibid.
7   Peter Leon, Webber Wentzel Law Firm, in 'How "contagious" is resource nationalism in Africa?' by Trish Saywell, 2013, in *The Northern Miner*, 13 March. Available at: www.northernminer.com [Accessed May 2014].

However, nationalisation is less clear when state action that interferes with an investor's property rights 'crosses the line' from otherwise valid regulation to compensable taking, often referred to as 'creeping', 'indirect' expropriation or 'stealth' nationalisation. The type of state actions taken in these instances is very similar to nationalism policy tools (described in detail below), but taken to the absolute extreme, restricting the foreign investor's operations to such a degree that they (the policy tools) substantially impair the value of the investment and/or effectively render it economically unfeasible or render the government actions as confiscatory. Creeping expropriation can include increasing regulatory compliance, pecuniary taxes, shutting down of forex movements, increasing focus on windfall taxes, manipulation of exchange rates, and enforced renegotiation. Expropriation – the taking of privately owned property by a government for public use or national interest – can occur directly or indirectly, with or without compensation.[8]

Increased Local Equity/Indigenisation

Indigenisation and local equity requirements can come under two guises: namely, government or private equity participation by locals in resource companies or projects.

Government equity participations in resource development projects have long been a feature of the mining industry, particularly in Africa. In addition to straightforward government equity participations, which are paid for to some degree, is the legislative requirement for government to receive a 'Free-Carried Interest'. This occurs when the government acquires free equity participation, usually of a non-dilutable nature.

Private local equity participation can occur through the direct sale of equity to private individuals and/or the distribution/sale of equity to local communities, workers and/or management.

Both government and private participations are generally viewed positively from a political perspective, but government equity participations are increasingly being considered by governments as a means to extract economic benefit, enable social transformation, obtain a measure of control, and a means of knowledge transfer.[9]

---

8   Philip Hill, David Lewis, James Pay, Audley Sheppard and Jo Delaney of Clifford Chance LLP, with PLC Finance. 2012. 'Resource Nationalism: A Return to the Bad Old Days?', Practical Law Company. Available at: www.practicallaw.com [Accessed May 2014].

9   Tanneke Heersche of Fasken Martineau DuMoulin LLP, South Africa. 2011. In 'Making Mines Work Harder – Resource Nationalism Trends in Africa', November, in *Who'sWhoLegal*. Available at: http://whoswholegal.com/news/features/article/29397/ [Accessed May 2014].

Royalties and Taxes

Mineral royalties and tax streams can constitute a significant source of revenue for state coffers. Given the fact that many developing countries are resource rich, yet cash poor, increasing taxes and royalties applicable to mining operations is one of the most effective means of extracting both greater immediate and longer-term financial benefits from mineral resources in order to boost national treasuries. Amending fiscal regimes, including tax legislation, has been undertaken in numerous jurisdictions throughout the world. This is often done in conjunction with broader socio-economic development initiatives.[10]

Policy and/or Legislative review

Governments have become increasingly aware of the need to regularly re-evaluate their policies and regulatory frameworks in respect of the mining industry in order to ensure the continued development of their resources on a secure and transparent basis whilst integrating socio-economic developmental and infrastructure needs. Thus, the scope of policy reviews extends to issues such as:

* logistics and power infrastructure development;
* development of associated industries through local beneficiation;
* local procurement;
* creating an enabling environment for enterprise development and investment;
* provision of linkages and investment along the mining supply chain;
* ensuring local companies have full and reasonable access to tenders and other opportunities;
* promoting the growth of the small-scale mining sector (in some countries); and
* corporate social responsibility providing direct social benefits to affected communities and regions, and sustainable development.[11]

Increased Oversight and Government Capacity

In many jurisdictions, government resources and capacity continue to be a significant challenge, if not a hindrance, in the implementation and enforcement of increasingly complex and integrated regulations and procedures. A well-developed and thought out regulatory environment is not sufficient if the government support structures and mechanisms required to implement and enforce such frameworks are not developed in parallel.[12]

---

10   Tanneke Heersche of Fasken Martineau DuMoulin LLP. 2011. 'South Africa Making Mines Work Harder – Resource Nationalism Trends in Africa', November. In *Who'sWhoLegal*. Available at: http://whoswholegal.com/news/features/article/29397/ [Accessed May 2014].

11   Ibid.

12   Ibid.

Contract Reviews

Contract reviews can include a variety of amendments to instigate contractual obligations on mining corporations in order to achieve government's required resource nationalism objectives. The types of amendments include, but are not limited to, the following:

* adjusting or cancelling stabilisation clauses and development agreements;
* adjusting tax and royalty payments; and
* re-negotiating contracts given that investment agreements in the extractive industry (mining and oil exploration) usually involve long-term concessions or mining licences that provide for flat royalty and tax rates. Often these agreements are regarded as unfair or not sufficiently beneficial to the host country.[13]

The report concludes that the phenomenon of resource nationalism is indeed a reality and is likely to continue for as long as the drivers persist. However, the nature and form of resource nationalism in the twenty-first century varies from the previous forms witnessed in the period after the Russian Revolution.

The main argument of the report is that private actors need to enter mining jurisdiction with a flexible approach that is able to create a win-win situation for all; some kind of a partnership akin to a social compact. After the failure of neoliberal prescriptions from the International Monetary Fund (IMF) and the World Bank, and the recent Global Financial Crisis (GFC) of 2008, private sector role players need to re-examine their business approach and reposition themselves in ways that appreciate the need to improve the human condition whilst making reasonable returns.

*Please note that all references to tonnage are metric, e.g. 1,000 kg.

---

13   Philip Hill, David Lewis, James Pay, Audley Sheppard and Jo Delaney of Clifford Chance LLP, with PLC Finance. 2012. 'Resource Nationalism: A Return to the Bad Old Days?', Practical Law Company. Available at: www.practicallaw.com [Accessed May 2104].

CHAPTER 2: AFRICA

INTRODUCTION

> *Resource Nationalism is characterised by the tendency of states to take or seek to take direct and increasing financial, regulatory and sometimes operational control of the economic activity in the natural resources sector. It is important to remember that nationalism is 'not new in global economic evolution' and it is important that extremes do not define approaches or policy responses for what has historically been a relatively everyday phenomena – the state has always had a vested interest in maximising benefits from its natural resources.*[14]

Resource nationalism has traditionally been understood as an effect of upward commodity price curves, a symptom of backlash against former colonial rule and/or anti-market ideology. This may have been correct in the 1970s, but in present times, resource nationalism is driven by a far more complex interaction of factors – all of which typically culminate in the state coming to the conclusion that foreign investors are getting too good a deal for their investment in comparison to the benefits experienced by the country.[15]

Actions regarded as 'resource nationalistic' have thus varied widely: from outright expropriation to tax hikes; through demand for greater state equity and indigenous participation to renegotiation of stability clauses in mining contracts. Also, so-called beneficiation strategies involve demands for value-added processing before exporting. Added to this, there are additional demands placed on companies such as community development, local procurement, technology transfer, skills development and training, environmental protection, and the broad concept of social licence to operate.[16]

Thus, although straightforward, nationalisation is no longer a regular occurrence: the boom in the demand for minerals over the last decade has encouraged an increase in resource nationalism in more 'subtle' forms in the developed and the developing world. As stated in *The Economist*, February 2012:

---

14   Dr Oladiran Bello, Head of the Governance of Africa's Resources Programme at the South African Institute of International Affairs (SAIIA). 2013. 'Resource nationalism threatens Africa's mining boom', 3 February. Available at: http://www.saiia.org.za/opinion-analysis/resource-nationalism-threatens-africas-mining-boom [Accessed 15 May 2014].

15   Philip Hill, David Lewis, James Pay, Audley Sheppard and Jo Delaney of Clifford Chance LLP, with PLC Finance. 2012. 'Resource Nationalism: A Return to the Bad Old Days?' Practical Law Company. Available at: www.practicallaw.com [Accessed 15 May 2014].

16   Dr Oladiran Bello, Head of the Governance of Africa's Resources Programme at the South African Institute of International Affairs (SAIIA). 2013. 'Resource nationalism threatens Africa's mining boom', 3 February. Available at: http://www.saiia.org.za/opinion-analysis/resource-nationalism-threatens-africas-mining-boom [Accessed 17 May 2014].

'The new resource nationalists, however, have embraced capitalism and shifted industry. Few governments think they can do a better job of extracting the minerals themselves; they just want a bigger pay-off from those whom they allow to do the mining.'[17]

In particular, the year 2011 saw a new 'resource nationalistic' drive with many countries actively taking steps to increase the benefits they derived from their natural resources. This has continued until today. According to Dr Jacek Guzek, a consultant with Deloitte and Touche South Africa, 25 out of 52 surveyed African countries have implemented resource nationalistic policies in one form or the other.[18]

BOTSWANA

Economic Context

At independence, Botswana was one of the poorest countries in Africa and was ranked among the least developed countries of the world. Thirty years later, Botswana has transformed itself into an upper-middle-income country and into one of the fastest-growing economies in the world, with an average annual growth rate of about nine per cent between 1966 and 1999. This is largely due to mineral (diamond) discoveries, causing Botswana to become the world's largest producer of diamonds.

Its diamond sector continues to be the mainstay of the economy, accounting for approximately one-third of the country's GDP, more than 45 per cent of government revenue, and about 70 per cent of export earnings. The government is acutely aware of the finite nature of its diamond resources and over the years has put in place policies to reduce its economic dependence on diamonds, seeing diversification out of diamonds as a priority. Main actions include accumulating funds for the future, building infrastructure and investing in health and education. Revenues from diamonds have been used effectively, with investment in public goods, social development and infrastructure. The government also took measures to boost productivity by limiting parastatals and promoting import substitution policies, made efforts to promote economic diversification, and pursued policies that avoided commodity and financial volatility by disassociating public expenditure from revenue.

In spite of these policies, the country has continued to face challenges related

17 *The Economist*. 2012. 'Resource nationalism in Africa: More for my people', 11 February. Available at: http://www.economist.com/node/21547246 [Accessed 17 May 2014].

18 Wesley Nkwazi and Phillip T. Shingira. 2013. 'The Next Frontier: Resource Nationalism in Africa', *The Trade Beat*, 4 June. Available at: http://www.thetradebeat.com/news-announcements/the-next-frontier-resource-nationalism-in-africa [Accessed 18 May 2014].

to its overdependence on the mining sector, and in 2011 the national budget was in deficit for the first time since independence. The World Bank has urged the government to slash its bloated public workforce (accounting for 40 per cent of formal jobs) by one quarter.

Among other major challenges confronting the government of Botswana is the national unemployment rate of 17.5 per cent, a poverty rate higher than 20 per cent and high income inequality.

Mining/energy sector

Botswana is the world's leading producer of diamonds by value, with the majority of its diamond production being of gem quality. Botswana's entire diamond production comes from Debswana, a 50/50 joint venture diamond company owned by the Botswana government and De Beers Consolidated Mines, established over 30 years ago.

Coal is becoming another significant resource for Botswana. At present, there is only one coal mine, Morupule Colliery, a 100 per cent subsidiary of Debswana. From a presentation given by Boikobo Paya, Permanent Secretary, Ministry of Minerals, Energy and Water Resources, it appears that Botswana coal's strategic roadmap underwent thorough investigation with regard to how best to exploit these reserves in a way that will meet the socio-economic and energy needs of the country in addition to diversifying the economy from heavy reliance on diamonds. Another objective of the roadmap was to ensure that investors are given more confidence around their long-term strategy and implementation plans.

Botswana's other significant, though smaller, mineral resources are copper, gold, nickel and soda ash production and processing. Together they make a notable contribution to the national economy.

Sector regulation

In Botswana, mineral rights are vested in the state. There are no restrictions on foreign ownership, although the payment of royalties is required. While the government retains the right to acquire a minority interest in new mines, this is up to a maximum of 15 per cent and is on commercial terms with the government paying its pro-rata share of costs incurred.

To make Botswana a more investor-friendly country, the government is reviewing pieces of legislation such as the Income Tax Act, the Mines and Minerals Act and the Diamond Cutting and Polishing Act.

Minerals Policy Objectives & Pillars (including but not limited to):

Resurgent Resource Nationalism? A Study Into The Global Phenomenon | Africa

17

* Maximise the economic benefits for the nation while enabling private investors to earn competitive returns.
* Create a competitive environment to stimulate private sector investment in mineral exploration and exploitation.
* Encourage linkages with the rest of the economy to expand value addition activities.
* Generate employment and training for Botswana's citizens.
* Protection of private property rights and accepting foreign investors as an integral part of the business community as well as their entitlement to make and repatriate profits.

Resource nationalism activity

The only 'act' of resource nationalism occurred in September 2012 when Botswana obliged De Beers Consolidated Mines to move its London-based sorting operation to Botswana – and all the jobs and other economic benefits that go with it – in return for an extension of the renegotiating period for its diamond-sales agreement from five to ten years.[19]

In fact, at present there is no hint of resource nationalism within Botswana. This is largely due to the fact that Botswana very cleverly ensured the nationalisation of its most important resource right at the beginning through its 50 per cent shareholding in Debswana.

GHANA

Economic Context

Ghana's GDP growth has been robust and impressive for the last ten years. In 2012, the growth was estimated at 7.1 per cent. It was even better the year before as it reached 14.4 per cent. The peak of high growth in 2011 was due to the start-up of oil production in the last quarter of 2010.

In general, GDP growth is driven by oil revenues, the services sector and the strong export performance of cocoa and gold. Ghana's medium-term growth outlook remains positive, thanks to large investments in the extractive industries, public infrastructure and commercial agriculture.[20]

Improved macro-economic management and enduring political stability have not significantly transformed the structure of Ghana's economy. The economic

---

19 *The Economist.* 2012. 'Resource nationalism in Africa: More for my people', 11 February. Available at: http://www.economist.com/node/21547246 [Accessed 10 May 2014].

20 *African Economic Outlook 2013, Structural Transformation and Natural Resources,* 'Country Notes – Ghana'. OECD. Available at: http://www.oecd-ilibrary.org/ [Accessed 15 May 2014].

transformation process is held hostage by a weakening agricultural sector, high labour and electricity costs. Ghana's land tenure issues deter investments in productive commercial agriculture. For this reason, domestic demand is met through cheaper imports.

Going forward, the country needs to tackle unemployment and the lack of economic opportunities in rural areas where poverty is endemic.

Mining/energy sector

Ghana has sizeable mineral deposits, crude oil reserves, natural gas and gold. It is one of the world's top 10 gold producers and the second largest in Africa, with gold being a key industry for Ghana's economy. Other mineral commodities produced in the country include diamonds, bauxite, manganese, salt and silver. In 2004, Ghana discovered offshore oil and gas, with commercial oil production starting in 2010. The government aims to diversify its minerals base into limestone, aggregates, clay and base metals.

Over the past decade, the mining sector has consistently been the highest gross foreign exchange earner. Mining royalties currently contribute up to 80 per cent of mining revenues compared to corporate taxes' 15 per cent. Implementation of a more balanced minerals revenue fiscal framework is hindered by capacity constraints in the Ghana Revenue Authority and asymmetrical information.[21]

Ghana discovered offshore oil and gas in 2004. Commercial oil production was scheduled to start in 2010 and actual production began in the first quarter of 2011. The Ghana National Petroleum Corporation (GNPC) is responsible for the commercial exploitation and exploration of Ghana's oil reserves. GNPC states that government intends to keep minority equity stakes ranging from five per cent to 10 per cent in all exploration activities.

Sector regulation

Ghana's Constitution and its Minerals and Mining Law state that all minerals are the property of the country and the president holds them in trust for the people. The mining industry in Ghana is overseen by the Ministry of Lands and Natural Resources and regulated by the Minerals Commission which was established under the Minerals Commission Act 1993. The Commission is responsible for the regulation and management of the mineral resources of Ghana and the coordination and implementation of mining policies.

---

21   *African Economic Outlook 2013, Structural Transformation and Natural Resources,* 'Country Notes – Ghana'. OECD. Available at: http://www.oecd-ilibrary.org/ [Accessed 15 May 2014].

Between 1986 and 2006, the Mineral and Mining Law 1986 was the basic mining legislation in Ghana. The 1986 Act was revised and enacted in 2006 (Minerals and Mining Act 2006). The 2006 Act was intended to reflect contemporary trends in minerals and mining legislation in order to position Ghana to continue to attract and retain mining investment. This was achieved by, but not limited to, the following amendments to the 1986 Act:

* Royalties were increased from three to 12 per cent, leading to total revenue increasing from three to six per cent of total minerals revenue obtained.
* Government's free 'carried interest' reduced from 20 per cent down to a maximum of 10 per cent (with respect to a mining lease only). Any further participation is to be on terms agreed with the holder.
* Foreign ownership limitations: there are no restrictions regarding foreign ownership except in respect to small-scale mining and restricted/industrial mineral operations, which are reserved for Ghanaians. In the case of the latter, foreigners can participate if their proposed investment is at least US$10 million.[22]

The Petroleum Exploration and Production Law 1984 (the Petroleum Law) regulates oil and gas exploration and production in Ghana. The law deals extensively with petroleum contracts, the rights, duties, responsibilities of contractors, and compensation payable to those affected by activities in the petroleum sector. A revision of the Petroleum Law regarding exploration and production is ongoing.

Ghana's Petroleum Revenue Management Act (2010) manages revenues generated by this industry. This law outlines clear mechanisms for collecting and distributing petroleum revenue. It specifies what percentage should help fund the annual budget, what should be set aside for future generations, and what should be invested for long-term benefits.

Resource nationalism activity

The 2010 revision of the mining code, Minerals and Mining (Amendment) Act 2010, included the following key revisions:

* renegotiation of stability agreements;
* a five per cent flat-rate royalty (compared to the three to six per cent range); and
* an increase in corporate tax from 25 to 35 per cent.

These revisions were put in place to increase government's tax earnings from the minerals industry. In 2011, the Finance Minister, Kwabena Duffuor,

---

22   United Nations. Available at: http://www.un.org/esa/dsd/dsd_aofw_ni/ni_pdfs/NationalReports/ghana/Mining.pdf [Accessed 25 April 2014].

was reported as saying that the ministry was in talks with gold miners in the country regarding the introduction of additional taxes, including the possible introduction of a windfall tax, so as to ensure that Ghana benefits from the soaring price of gold.[23]

In the 2012 Budget Statement, government upped the corporate mining tax from 25 per cent to 35 per cent, announced a windfall tax of 10 per cent and established a uniform regime for capital allowance of 20 per cent (down from 80 per cent) over a five-year period. However, the windfall tax had not yet received parliamentary approval at the end of the first quarter of 2013:[24]

* *The government established a committee to review its mine development agreements with companies in February 2012, with the mandate of renegotiating agreements that are not in Ghana's best interests.*
* *Some civil society organisations have called on government, as a matter of urgency, to review the Minerals and Mining Act because the Act is disadvantageous to the country, saying the Minerals and Mining Act 2006, as it stands now, provides incentives to mining investors and denies government the opportunity to accrue enough revenue from the mining sector. They blamed the situation on the generous incentives government grants to mining investors at the expense of the populace, and which incentives only served to attract foreign miners to deplete the country's mineral resources at a rapid rate. It was proposed that in a bid to ensure retention of capital in the country, it is proposed that the percentage of earnings that could be kept offshore should not be above 50 per cent.*[25]

MOZAMBIQUE

Economic context

Mozambique is one of the rising economies on the African continent, achieving an average annual GDP growth rate of 7.2 per cent during the last decade, despite having one of the lowest human development indexes in the world. Drivers of growth include large-scale projects (megaprojects) in the extractive and energy industries, continuation of sizable foreign direct investment (FDI) inflows, increased coal production, credit expansion to the private sector, strong infrastructure investment, and development of services around mining projects.[26]

Agriculture remains a vital aspect of the economy, accounting for nearly 80 per

23   Tanneke Heersche of Fasken Martineau DuMoulin LLP, South Africa. 2011. 'Making Mines Work Harder – Resource Nationalism Trends in Africa', November. In *Who'sWhoLegal*, http://whoswholegal.com/news/features/article/29397/ [Accessed 15 April 2014].

24   Samuel Boadi. 2013. *Daily Guide Ghana*, 3 February. [Accessed 15 April 2014].

25   *Ghana News*. 2013. Available at: spyghana.com, 7 February. [Accessed 15 April 2014].

26   *African Economic Outlook 2013, Structural Transformation and Natural Resources*, 'Mozambique'. OECD. Available at: http://www.oecd-ilibrary.org/ [Accessed 12 May 2014].

cent of employment. In 2012, it experienced a relatively modest growth rate of 3.4 per cent and an estimated 3.7 per cent in 2013.

Mozambique's productive base remains largely dependent on natural resources which are concentrated in a few megaprojects. These megaprojects have resulted in large FDI inflows, which have driven economic growth but have not had a significant impact on government revenues, employment creation and economic diversification.

Weak human capital, high cost of credit, deficient infrastructure and burdensome regulations have slowed the diversification of the economic structure.[27] This, in spite of attempts to stimulate linkages between small and medium size enterprises and foreign investment, as well as providing incentives to labour-intensive sectors. Poverty remains widespread, with more than 50 per cent of Mozambicans living on less than US$1 a day. In addition, the growing gap between rich and poor is causing tension.

Mining/energy sector
In recent years, Mozambique has emerged as a resource haven. In addition to rich deposits of coal and natural gas, Mozambique has significant deposits of heavy mineral sands, limestone, bauxite, gold, and base minerals, among others.

The main mineral resources currently being produced on a large scale are natural gas, coal and titanium products. Gold, precious and semiprecious stones, are being produced, mainly at the level of small-scale and artisanal mining.

Sector regulation
Under the Mozambique Constitution, the government owns all mineral resources in the soil, subsoil, in interior waters and in the territorial sea, on the continental shelf, and in the exclusive economic zone. Further, land is the property of the state and can be used on a lease basis. The maximum period of a land lease is 50 years and can be renewable for a further 50 years.

The Ministry of Mineral Resources (MMR) is the supervising entity for the mining sector in Mozambique. The ministry supervises the application of the government mining legislation through its subdivisions; in particular, the National Directorate of Mines. Mining rights are issued on a first come, first served, basis. The mining regime does not differentiate national entities from foreign entities, except in respect of artisanal and small-scale mining, which licences are exclusively for Mozambicans.

---

27   Ibid.

Although there are currently no requirements for ownership by indigenous persons/entities directly imposed by law, the state has a principle to include provisions in the concession contracts that govern the empowerment of local entrepreneurs/entities.[28]

The Ministry of Mineral Resources is vested with powers to administer or regulate the exploration and production of oil and gas. The National Petroleum Institute (NIP) is the regulatory authority responsible for:

* petroleum operations of exploration, production and transport of hydrocarbons;
* the promotion and negotiation of any petroleum concession contracts on behalf of the government; and
* the organisation of tenders for the award of exploration and prospecting concessions.

The current legislation allows the government the right to participate in petroleum operations: the state oil company, National Hydrocarbon Corporation (ENH), participates in exploration with carried interest in association with oil companies, and reserves the right to be a stakeholder in the natural gas project.

Resource nationalism activity

In 2012, the Ministry of Mineral Resources and Energy in Mozambique issued a tender for new exploration licences in the coal-rich Tete province that was restricted to Mozambicans only.[29]

In 2013, Mozambique was reportedly set to introduce a fixed 32 per cent capital gains tax rate on the sale of local assets by foreign companies from January 2014, according to a Mozambican tax official. Rosario Fernandes, the head of the national tax authority, has said, 'Come 1 January, capital gains in all mega projects, including oil and gas, will be taxed according to the new legislation.'[30]

The Mozambican Tax Authority (AT) has indicated a Sovereign Wealth Fund as one possible destination for the large sums of money raised from the above-mentioned capital gains tax on transactions involving the country's mineral resources. However, Custudio Nguetana, the spokesperson for the meeting of the Coordinating Council of the Ministry of Mineral Resources, remained

---

28   Mozambique Mining Legislation. Available at: http://www.iclg.co.uk/practice-areas/mining-law/mining-law-2014/mozambique [Accessed 11 May 2014].
29   Ernst & Young. 2012. 'Resource Nationalism Update', June. Available at: http://www.ey.com/Publication/ [Accessed 15 May 2014].
30   Ibid.

sceptical, stating that solving the problems with health and education and building up the country's infrastructure had to be dealt with 'before we put money in the bank'. (For example, the sale of shares in the Rovuma Basin Area Four, where much of the recent gas discoveries have been made, netted the Mozambican government US$400 million in capital gains tax.[31]

Since 2002, Mozambique has had a liberal mining law that helped attract inward investment. New laws introduced in 2011 and 2012 demonstrate a refreshing approach to resource nationalism. Large mining firms must make available to the Mozambican public between five per cent and 20 per cent of their equity via the Mozambican stock exchange on commercial terms. Rather than taxing windfall profits, Mozambique requires that they be held in reserve against losses or reinvested in Mozambique.

TANZANIA

Economic context
Over the past few years, Tanzania's economy has been following a steady GDP growth path in a low and stable inflation rate environment. For instance, GDP growth was 6.4 per cent in 2011, estimated at 6.8 per cent in 2012, projected at 6.9 per cent in 2013 and is expected to average at seven per cent in the medium term. Tanzania's maintenance of overall macroeconomic stability, combined with institutional and policy reforms, has been a major contributor to this growth, along with a steady increase in domestic demand (the result of rapid population growth). Over and above that, telecommunications, transport, construction and trade contributed to Tanzania's economic growth. The mineral resources sector played a significant role, particularly gold. It has been a major source of industrial production and strong export performance over the years.

Despite its real GDP growth, the structure of Tanzania's economy, whilst changed, has not significantly transformed, and the expected broad-based wealth creation and poverty reduction have been disappointing (poverty levels are at approximately 33 per cent overall and 42 per cent of the population is under 15 years of age). A host of strategies to reduce poverty remain weakly implemented due to capacity constraints, low political will and commitment.

Moreover, the country is experiencing substantial infrastructure development challenges, and these are retarding Tanzania's economic growth. Some of the

---

31   *allAfrica*. 2013. 'Mozambique: Mineral Ministry Skeptical About Sovereign Fund', 8 September. Available at: http://allafrica.com/stories/201309090426.html [Accessed 15 May 2014].

challenges include infrastructure bottlenecks, a chronic energy crisis and high dependence on external aid. In 2010, the ratio of external aid was 14 per cent of GDP.

Additionally, Tanzania has remained predominantly an agrarian economy, but the sector is underperforming. It contributes only 23.7 per cent to GDP whilst employing over 75 per cent of the country's workforce.

The newly-found natural gas reserves have significantly enhanced Tanzania's medium-term growth prospects and may well propel the transformation of Tanzania's socio-economic position if the fiscal revenues therefrom are managed wisely, ensuring inclusive sharing of gains and benefits.

Mining/energy sector

Tanzania is Africa's third largest gold producer. Other known mineral resources include coal, diamonds, iron ore, tanzanite, graphite, phosphate, rubies, limestone, platinum group metals (PGMs) and uranium.

Tanzania commenced commercial gas production in 2004, major new discoveries were then made in 2012, and explorations are ongoing. This, combined with new mineral discoveries, is expected to boost the extractive industry growth. Although some degree of uncertainty surrounds the level of expected revenue, the proven natural gas reserves could earn up to an estimated US$2.5 billion a year – 46 per cent of Tanzania's estimated total fiscal revenue for 2012/13 – with revenue from newly found gas reserves flowing in over 2020–40.[32]

In 2012, Tanzania drafted a Natural Gas Policy to guide the development of the gas industry to ensure that benefits are maximised and contribute to economic transformation. In order to achieve this, an extensive upgrading of the country's legal and institutional frameworks, strengthening transparency and accountability, and the establishment of open mechanisms for contract scrutiny will be required.

Sector regulation

The Government of Tanzania retains ownership of all natural resources. Foreign investment is welcomed with no restrictions on foreign ownership, other than for small-scale mining licenses and gemstone mining, where a foreign investor may be required to partner with a national company.

---

32 *African Economic Outlook 2013, Structural Transformation and Natural Resources*, 'Tanzania'. OECD. Available at: http://www.oecd-ilibrary.org/ [Accessed 20 May 2014].

The mining industry in Tanzania is regulated at a national level and the main regulatory body responsible for the mining industry is the Ministry of Energy and Minerals (MEM). There is a Commissioner for Minerals ('the Commissioner') within the MEM appointed by the President; the Commissioner supervises and regulates the proper and effectual carrying out of the provisions of the Mining Act 2010. There is also a Mining Advisory Committee constituted, pursuant to the Mining Act, which is responsible for advising the Minister on matters concerning the mining sector.[33]

The Mining Act 2010 introduced significant changes to mining policy and to its predecessor, the Mining Act 1998. These included:

*   Gemstone licences only to be granted to Tanzanians, except where the minister determines that the development is most likely to require specialised skills, technology or a high level of investment, in which case the licence may be granted to an applicant so long as the non-Tanzanian participation element is no more than 50 per cent.
*   Free carry interest and state equity participation: The Act gives the minister power to make regulations authorising government to participate in the conduct and financing of mining operations and gives the government a free carried interest, the level of which is not set by statute, but rather by negotiation between government and the relevant mineral rights holder.
*   Royalties: It amends the method by which royalties are calculated so that they will, in future, be levied on the gross value of minerals, rather than the present method of calculation which refers to the net value.

Resource nationalism activity

Since 1985, the Government of Tanzania has not expropriated any foreign investments. Resource nationalism is mostly occurring in the form of policy and legislative amendments and mining contract reviews:

*   Review of mining contracts: The government conducted an in-depth review of mining contracts in 2006 to assess why revenue from mining activities was so small. As a result, contracts were re-negotiated, companies were required to pay US$200,000 annually to local authorities, in addition to a three per cent royalty to the central government on the value of exports.[34]
*   The Bomani Commission: Another important milestone was the formation in 2007 of the Presidential Mining Review Committee, known as the Bomani

33   Peter Kasanda, Teresa Hettich and Carl Hotton. 2013. 'Renewal of a Prospecting Licence: Key Considerations', *Tanzania Mining Briefing*, June. Tanzania: Clyde & Co. Available at: http://www.mondaq.com/x/250416/Mining/Tanzania+Mining+Briefing+Renewal+Of+A+Prospecting+Licence+Key+Considerations+June+2013 [Accessed 20 May 2014].

34   Silas Olan'g. 2010. 'Tanzania Passes a New Mining Law and Builds Capacity for Informed Policy Debate', Revenue Watch Institute, 21 May. Available at: http://www.revenuewatch.org/news/ [Accessed 20 May 2014].

Commision. Some of the commission's recommendations informed new mining policy of 2009 and the newly-passed 2010 law.[35]

* The Mining Act 2010: (the 'Mining Act'): The Act came into effect in the wake of public concerns at what the citizenry was getting out of the mining sector and the meagre royalties the government was getting. The gap between the sector's financial success and its uncertain benefit to citizens' lives has made the national role of mining highly controversial. For over a decade, many Tanzanians have believed the sector disproportionately benefits foreign mining companies. This climate of distrust has only been exacerbated by the fact that the mining contracts and development agreements have been withheld from public scrutiny, and by the government's recent failure to enforce environmental law.[36]

* Imposition of a levy: In 2011, Tanzanian lawmakers approved a US$27.4 billion economic development plan (EDP) which proposes the imposition of a levy on 'super-profits' from mining in order to fund the EDP.

* Increasing royalty payments: Government engaged directly in talks with mining companies to negotiate the Mining Act 2010's increased royalty payments on exports of key minerals from three to four per cent. Minerals and Energy Minister, William Ngela, was reported as saying that the government had reached substantial agreement with mining companies and that they accordingly expect the migration to the new rates to have commenced by the end of 2011.[37]

In 2013, Tanzanian Energy and Minerals Minister, Sospeter Muhongo, announced on 30 August that the 13 largest foreign mining companies would need to comply with a new local content regulation, requiring them to procure at least 80 per cent of goods and services from local businesses by 2015.

Government statistics report that large-scale miners spent US$1.4 billion on procurement in 2012, although only 38.6 per cent was procured locally. Consequently, the government has drawn up a list of goods and services that can be procured locally, including food supplies, engineering, logistics and legal services. The new policy and future regulations are an attempt to satisfy growing calls from local MPs for greater revenue to be extracted from mining companies and to apply existing mining laws more stringently.[38]

---

35   Ibid.

36   Ibid.

37   Tanneke Heersche of Fasken Martineau DuMoulin LLP. 2011. 'South Africa Making Mines Work Harder-Resource Nationalism Trends in Africa', November, in *Who'sWhoLegal*. Available at: http://whoswholegal.com/news/features/article/29397/ [Accesed 20 May 2014].

38   Ernst & Young. 2013. 'Resource Nationalism Update', October. Available at: http://www.ey.com/Publication/vwLUAssets/EY-M-and-M-Resource-nationalism-update-October-2013/US$FILE/EY-M-and-M-Resource-nationalism-update-October-2013.pdf [Accessed 20 May 2014].

ZAMBIA

Economic context

Zambia's economic growth over the last decade has been robust, averaging around six per cent (2012: 7.3 per cent; 2013: 7.5 per cent; 2014: 7.8 per cent). Growth has been boosted by economic liberalisation, privatisation and the resource boom, specifically in copper mining. The strong performance was expected to continue in 2014, premised on increased mining output, rising construction activity and sustained robust growth in services and agriculture.

Zambia's economy continues to rely on the copper industry, which accounts for about 80 per cent of foreign exchange earnings and only six per cent of total revenues. Nonetheless, growth was also driven by expansion in agriculture, construction, manufacturing, transport and finance. Mining growth faltered in 2012 due to labour strikes and policy uncertainty following elections in 2011.[39]

Zambia's growth will remain redundant unless there is a corresponding increase in job creation, and progress in poverty reduction and further progress in tackling the HIV and Aids pandemic. Zambia's natural resources have not been harnessed to foster structural transformation and inclusive job creation. In spite of Zambia's mineral resource boom (driven, in part, by high international prices), the revenue effect has been weak, exacerbated by the lopsided mineral fiscal regime, which, until 2008, favoured foreign investors.[40]

Zambia's abundance in natural resources and water (it is believed that Zambia accounts for about 60 per cent of the water resources in southern Africa) do present numerous opportunities for economic transformation. Further, apart from providing fiscal benefits, copper mining can lead the way to Zambia's greater industrialisation. Satellite SMEs supporting the mining industry are already in place. The potential for agriculture to contribute to structural transformation is immense. Currently, agriculture contributes seven per cent of GDP growth and employs an estimated 85 per cent of the workforce, mostly in the subsistence sector. However, productivity is very low; agriculture only contributes five per cent of total merchandise exports, and the linkages with manufacturing are generally weak. The major hindrance to improved agriculture and livestock productivity is investment in infrastructure and lack of extension services, particularly to small-scale farmers.[41]

39   Ernst & Young. 2013. 'Resource Nationalism Update', October. Available at: http://www.ey.com/Publication/vwLUAssets/EY-M-and-M-Resource-nationalism-update-October-2013/US$FILE/EY-M-and-M-Resource-nationalism-update-October-2013.pdf [Accessed 20 May 2014].

40   Ibid.

41   Ibid.

Poverty is widespread, life expectancy is amongst the lowest in the world, and the death rate is one of the highest – largely due to the prevalence of HIV and Aids.

Constraints to Zambia's structural transformation result from Zambia's huge infrastructure deficit, burdensome regulatory and tax regime, limited access to finance, low level of skills, and the general high cost of doing business. There are indications of government commitment to pursuing diversification processes with policies focused on overcoming these constraints.[42]

Mining/energy sector

Zambia is richly endowed with copper. It is Africa's top copper producer and the world's seventh largest, making up approximately six per cent of global output. Zambia is further endowed with other substantial mineral resources which include cobalt, coal, uranium, nickel, lead, zinc, iron, manganese, gemstones, and a number of industrial minerals. Copper is the single largest contributor to the economy.[43]

Zambia Consolidated Copper Mines Ltd (ZCCM) once dominated the Zambian copper industry as the state mining company following the nationalisation of Anglo American Plc assets in the 1970s. In the end, ZCCM operated 10 mines, three smelters, two refineries and a tailings leach plant. In effect, ZCCM Ltd was a consolidated copper mining conglomerate majority, jointly owned by the government (60.3 per cent) and held by Zambia Copper Investments Ltd (ZCI) (27.3 per cent), an associate company of Anglo American Plc, with the balance held by private investors (12.4 per cent). The privatisation process involved the unbundling of its mining assets into several business units which it sold off. What remained is ZCCM Investment Holdings Plc (ZCCM-IH), which retained minority interests of not more than 21 per cent within each of the business units sold. ZCCM-IH principal activities include managing the Zambian government's stake in the mining sector. It is listed on the Lusaka Stock Exchange, the London Stock Exchange and on Euronext in Paris, and the majority of its investments are in the copper mining sector of Zambia. Currently, the company's shareholders are the government (87.6 per cent shareholding) and private equity holders (12.4 per cent).[44] In October 2013, it was reported that government plans to cede control of the company by cutting its 87.6 per cent to less than 50 per cent. Mines minister, Christopher Yaluma, said in this regard: '[w]e are not looking

---

42   *African Economic Outlook 2013, Structural Transformation and Natural Resources*, 'Zambia'. OECD. Available at: http://www.
      oecd-ilibrary.org/development/african-economic-outlook-2013_aeo-2013-en [Accessed 20 May 2014].

43   Ibid.

44   'Brief history of ZCCM-IH'. Available at: http://www.zccm-ih.com.zm [Accessed 18 May 2014].

back, but looking forward and getting the mining houses totally into private hands. We have gone past nationalisation and we are not going back'.[45]

Mining/energy sector

All rights of ownership of minerals are vested in the president on behalf of the republic. The Ministry of Mines and Minerals Development is responsible for enacting legislation for the mining sector in Zambia. The government does not participate in exploration or other mining activities, or in any shareholding activity other than in a regulatory and promotional role. The legislation is generally very favourable to investors.

The Mines and Minerals Development Act 2008 (replacing the Mines and Minerals Development Act 1995) made some noteworthy amendments as follows:

* Foreign Ownership: The only limitation to foreign ownership in the mining industry is in respect of a prospecting permit, small-scale mining licence, small-scale gemstone licence and an artisan's mining rights, which can only be granted to a Zambian citizen or Zambian-owned company.
* Preference for Zambian Products: It appears that, to promote economic growth and empowerment, the Act offers preferential treatment to Zambian products, materials and service agencies owned by Zambian citizens in the conduct of operations, under the mining right, or mineral processing licence, and in the purchase, construction and installation of facilities. The Act gives preference, to the maximum extent possible. Additionally, a licence or right holder is expected to give preference in employment to citizens of Zambia to the maximum extent possible.[46]

Resource nationalism activity

In 2011, Zambia introduced a 10 per cent levy on the export of ore as it sought to increase local value addition to mineral products. In 2012, royalties were doubled to six per cent per annum for base metals, and the corporate tax rate was increased for mining companies. In 2013, Zambia cancelled the operating licence for the Chinese-owned Collum Coal Mining in Sinazeze, thereby taking over operations through ZCCM-Investment Holdings.[47]

45   Matthew Hill. 2013. 'Zambia to cede control in copper mines', *Mail and Guardian*, 9 October. Available at: http://mg.co.za/article/2013-10-09-zambia-to-cede-control-in-copper-mines [Accessed 18 May 2014]

46   Africa Legal Network. Available at: http://www.africalegalnetwork.com/wp-content/uploads/2013/09/Zambia.pdf [Accessed 12 May 2014].

47   Maimbolwa Mulikelela. 2013. 'Zambia: Govt Takes Over Collum Coal Mine', *allAfrica.com*, 21 February. Available at: http://allafrica.com/stories/201302230173.html [Accessed 13 May 2014].

CONCLUSION

The economic uncertainty caused by changes in policy by the governments of resource-rich nations (which are sometimes abrupt and sudden) cannot be understated. The conundrum is to distinguish between governments engaged in resource nationalism and governments engaged in establishing a more equitable fiscal scenario. In terms of advice for investors on how best to navigate a resource nationalist landscape, the words of a Deloitte think-piece provide a good beginning: build mutual trust and interdependence in the countries in which operations occur. This incorporates operating in a way that promotes sustainable development.

Whilst governments should not be 'in hock' to multinationals, they must make decisions on mining consistently, competently and constructively: African governments must not wring so much out of their resources today that the mining companies fail to invest for the future. The art is in striking the right balance. The mining industry as a whole looks at Botswana enviously, wondering what went so right. Many analysts agree that Botswana's ability to avoid many of the mistakes of other countries in terms of nationalisation is due to the combination of good governance, a relatively homogenous population, a high degree of transparency, and prudent economic management involving significant investment in the socio-economic structures. But, actually, good governance is the main umbrella: the country's leadership deserves credit for designing and fostering conditions of governance that have ensured stability, respect for property rights and the rule of law. Other governments should take note.

CHAPTER 3: LATIN AMERICA

INTRODUCTION

According to Weisbrot (2006), the collapse of economic growth in the region after a turn to the right and the introduction of neo-liberal economic policies after 1980, was a major force behind – and perhaps the most important cause of – the sea-change in Latin American politics. The region had an era of successful economic growth from the post-war period to 1980. 'From 1960 to 1980, per capita income grew by 91.5 per cent, or an average of 3.3 per cent a year. Over the next 20 years, from 1980 to 2000, it grew by just 5.7 per cent, an average of 0.3 per cent a year. This was the worst long-term economic growth failure in Latin America for at least a century.'[48] As a result, the winning Left candidates during the 2000s ran explicitly against the neo-liberal policies, which were associated with the growth failure. For example, Venezuela was the fastest-growing economy in Latin America between 1920 and 1975, with a per capita GDP growth rate of four per cent. By 1977, Venezuela was by far the richest country in Latin America with a GDP per capita 2.1 times the regional average. However, between 1978 and 1998 (when Chavez was elected) GDP per capita declined by 21.5 per cent.[49]

In 2012, Latin America had a GDP of US$5,640 billion. South America, Mexico and Central America accounted for 76 per cent, 20.9 per cent and 3.2 per cent of the region's GDP respectively. The region had proven oil reserves of 338.2 billion barrels, equivalent to 20.3 per cent of the world's total. Venezuela, with proven oil reserves of almost 300 billion barrels, accounted for 88 per cent of the region's total, followed by Brazil with 4.5 per cent and Mexico with 3.4 per cent. Latin America produced 10 million barrels a day, equivalent to 11.6 per cent of world production. The major producers were Mexico (2.9 million barrels a day), Venezuela (2.7 million barrels a day) and Brazil (2.1 million barrels a day). The region also had proven natural gas reserves of 7.7 trillion cubic feet, equivalent to 4.1 per cent of the world's total.

Venezuela's proven natural gas reserves of 5.6 trillion cubic feet accounted for 73 per cent of the region's total. Total production was 190 billion cubic metres. The largest producers were Mexico (58.5 billion cubic feet), Argentina (37.7

48   M. Weisbrot. 2006. 'Latin America: the End of an Era', Centre for Economic Policy and Research. Available at: http://www.cepr. net/index.php/reports/latin-america-the-end-of-an-era/ [Accessed November 2013].

49   Kio Advisory Services. 2010. 'Harnessing South Africa's Mineral Resources for Economic Growth and Development: Lessons and Experiences From Abroad', South African Mining Development Association.

billion cubic feet) and Venezuela (32.8 billion cubic feet). Latin America had relatively small coal deposits (in Colombia, Brazil, Venezuela and Mexico) of 13 billion tonnes, equivalent to 1.5 per cent of the world's total. Production was 68 million tonnes, equivalent to about 1.8 per cent of the world total. Finally, in 2010, the region's metallic mineral production was US$113.6 billion with Brazil (US$47 billion), Chile (US$31.3 billion) and Peru (US$18.8 billion), accounting for 86 per cent of the world's total. Brazil and Chile were the world's third and fourth largest metallic mineral producers after Australia (US$72 billion) and China (US$69 billion).[50]

Since Central America has few natural resources, this analysis will focus on Mexico and South America. Over the past century, the region has veered between the extremes of state-led and neo-liberal economic development models, which influenced policies towards natural resources. According to Chua (1995), with few exceptions, countries in the region have been cycling back and forth between privatisation and nationalisation for as long as they have been independent. Latin America achieved independence from Spanish and Portuguese colonial rule during the first half of the nineteenth century. Following a period of political turbulence, most of the modern states of Central and South America took their present shape by 1880.

While conditions varied, the emergent governments embraced the institutions of late nineteenth century economic liberalism: private property regimes accompanied with laissez-faire policies and a huge dependence on foreign capital. Roughly, there was a postcolonial laissez faire period that was followed after 1930 by a new burst of revolutionary activity that gave rise to the first Latin American nationalisation programmes. That was followed by a return to privatisation in many countries, then a second cycle of nationalisation from the 1960s. During the 1980s, many countries went through another cycle of privatisation. By the early 1990s, most countries in the region had been through five privatisation-nationalisation cycles.[51] A close analysis of the case studies shows that the key issue in analysing performance of natural resource companies is not whether they are state-owned or private, but whether there are institutional mechanisms to ensure that there is adequate investment to maintain and increase production. There could be a case for fiscal rules or panels to ensure that governments do not raid the companies to the detriment of investment.

---

50 International Monetary Fund. 2013. 'Regional Economic Outlook: Western Hemisphere'. Available at: http://www.imf.org/external/pubs/ft/reo/2013/whd/eng/wreo0513.htm [Accessed November 2013].
BP Statistical Review of World Energy. 2013. Available at: http://www.bp.com/en/global/corporate/about-bp/statistical-review-of-world-energy-2013/statistical-review-downloads.html [Accessed November 2013].

51 A. Chua. 1995. 'The Privatization-Nationalization Cycle: The Link Between Markets and Ethnicity in Developing Countries', Yale Law School. Available at: http://digitalcommons.law.yale.edu/fss_papers/342/ [Accessed November 2013].

ARGENTINA

Argentina is South America's largest producer of natural gas and a significant producer of oil. The extractive regime involves 51 per cent state ownership of Yacimientos Petrolíferos Fiscales (YPF), the country's largest producer, with about a third of oil production and more than 20 per cent of gas output.[52] On a see-through basis, after excluding private shareholders in YPF, the state owns about 16.5 per cent of oil production and more than 10 per cent of gas output. Compared with other countries, Argentina has a high level of private participation in its oil and gas sector. The country's extractive regime also includes a royalty rate of 12 per cent[53] that goes to local governments, and an export tax, which allows the government to control the price of exports to guarantee domestic supply. Until recently, the government kept the difference between the international oil price and a reference price of US$42. In January 2013, the government increased the reference price to US$70, which will mean more income for companies that export crude oil.[54]

A century ago, Argentina was one of the world's 10 richest countries.[55] Since then, its performance has slipped to a position close to that of developing countries. The explanations for the so-called 'great retardation' differ on the reasons for, and the exact timing of, the decline. A brief overview shows that there was rapid growth of almost six per cent a year during the liberal Belle Epoque of 1870–1914, which slowed to a still respectable 3.8 per cent during the inter-war years from 1914 to 1929. During the years of state-led import substitution development strategies from 1930 to 1975, the economy grew at a more pedestrian, but not disastrous, annual average rate of 3.3 per cent. Then there was a collapse to an average of 0.1 per cent a year during the 'early economic liberalisation' phase from 1975 to 1990. Growth picked up to 3.6 per cent a year during the 'intense economic liberalisation' phase from 1990 to 2000.[56] But the neo-liberal reforms were discredited as they produced the country's worst-ever economic crisis when GDP dropped by 28 per cent from its peak in 1998 to its trough in 2002.[57] Since then, under left-wing governments, the economy recovered and grew by 94 per cent between 2002 and 2011.[58] Argentina was the

52 US Energy Information Administration. 2012. Argentina Country Brief. Available at: http://www.eia.gov/countries/analysisbriefs/cabs/Argentina/pdf.pdf [Accessed on 14 November 2013].

53 EY. 2013. *Global Oil and Gas Tax Guide 2013*.

54 Reuters. 2013. 'Argentina Cuts Oil Export Tax as it Seeks to Lure Investment', 7 January.

55 Prados de la Escosura and Sanz-Villarroya. 2004. 'Institutional Instability and Growth in Argentina: A Long-Run View', Universidad Carlos III De Madrid. Available at: http://econpapers.repec.org/paper/ctewhrepe/wh046705.htm [Accessed on 14 November 2013].

56 A. Solimano. 2003. 'Development Cycles, Political Regimes and International Migration: Argentina in the Twentieth Century', Economic Commission for Latin America and the Caribbean. Available at: http://www.cepal.org/publicaciones/xml/4/11854/lcl1847i.pdf [Accessed on 14 November 2013].

57 J. Saxton. 2003. 'Argentina's Economic Crisis: Causes and Cures', Joint Economic Committee, United States Congress. Available at: http://www.hacer.org/pdf/Schuler.pdf [Accessed 14 November 2013].

58 Weisbrot, Ray; Montecino and Kozameh. 2011. 'The Argentine Success Story and its Implications', Centre for Economic Policy

fastest-growing economy in Latin America between 2003 and 2012, with an annual average GDP growth rate of 7.2 per cent.

After 1989, when Carlos Menem became president, Argentina implemented a drastic neoliberal reform programme, which included wholesale privatisation across many sectors of the economy. The YPF restructuring started with auctions of portions of exploration rights in central and secondary fields and the sale of unprofitable physical assets, which netted the government more than US$2 billion. Massive retrenchments followed as the employee headcount was slashed from 51,000 in December 1990 to 8,000 in December 1993. The YPF's bottom line improved from a deficit of US$700 million in 1990 to a profit of more than US$500 million in 1992. The company was now ready for privatisation. In 1993, the government sold 45 per cent of the company's shares in a public offer to private investors for US$3 billion. The government retained a 20 per cent shareholding, but in addition had a golden share, which gave it the right to veto important decisions.[59]

At the time of its first privatisation, YPF held 46 per cent of the country's oil, 50 per cent of gas reserves, 43 per cent of oil production and 48 per cent of the downstream (retail) market, according to the *Oil and Gas Journal*.[60] In January 1999, the government sold 15 per cent of YPF to Repsol, the Spanish oil company, for US$2 billion. In May 1999, Repsol bought the remaining 85 per cent of shares for US$13.44 billion. In total, the government netted US$20 billion during the three share sales and the sale of exploration rights and physical assets. In 2008, the Argentinian Peterson Group paid US$2.24 billion for a 14.9 per cent shareholding in Repsol-YPF. In September 2011, it sold 16.57 per cent of its shares on the stock market. In 2011, the Peterson Group paid US$1.3 billion for another 10 per cent shareholding. After the three sales, Repsol had 57.43 per cent of the shares, the Peterson Group had 25.46 per cent and the remaining shares were a free-float, traded on the New York and Buenos Aires stock exchanges. Over the period 1999 to 2011, YPF's sales increased to US$56.7 billion from US$6.6 billion and its profit increased to US$5.3 billion from US$477 million.[61]

In April 2012, Argentina's president, Cristina Fernández de Kirchner, announced the expropriation of 51 per cent of the 57.43 per cent shares

---

Research. Available at: http://www.cepr.net/index.php/publications/reports/the-argentine-success-story-and-its-implications [Accessed 14 November 2013].

59   Sang-Hyun Yi. 2008. 'The Political Economy of Privatisation of YPF in Argentina', *Asian Journal of Latin American Studies*, Vol. 21, No. 3. Available at: http://www.ajlas.org/v2006/paper/2008vol21no304.pdf.

60   'Privatisation of State Company Catalyses Argentinian Oil Industry', *Oil & Gas Journal*, 13 February 1995.

61   P. R. José, E. Rodriguez Fernandez-Hidalgo, R. Costamagna and L. Susaeta. 2013. 'The Expropriation of Repsol-YPF', proceedings of the 2013 annual conference of the Business Association of Latin American Studies, Lima, Peru. Available at: http://www.balas.org/BALAS_2013_proceedings_data/data/20130321.html [Accessed 14 November 2013].

belonging to Repsol-YPF in a move that had huge popular support, including that of former president Menem, now a senator. The move was also criticised by many people for not going far enough and nationalising 100 per cent of the company.[62] 'We are the only country in Latin America, and I would say in practically the entire world, that doesn't manage its own natural resources,' she said.[63] Of the expropriated portion, national government would get 51 per cent and 10 oil-producing provinces would control the remaining 49 per cent. Repsol has demanded compensation of US$10.5 billion. The government accused the Spanish group of a lack of investment in exploration and production, thus causing shortages in the domestic market and contributing to the fuel trade deficit. The dividend distribution policy channelled funds mostly to foreign investors. For example, between 2008 and 2010, the company had earnings of US$12.92 billion and paid out US$14.91 billion in dividends.

Also, oil production fell by four per cent a year, and gas production by three per cent a year after Repsol's acquisition of YPF in 1999.[64] Argentinian oil production was about 500,000 bpd during the 1980s. During the 1990s, it increased steadily and peaked at a high of 910,000 bpd in 2001. After that, production decreased to 687,000 bpd in 2011 as demand soared 40 per cent between 2000 and 2010.[65] As a result, imports have soared, resulting in a rising trade deficit. However, the company reports that it invested US$1.36 billion in 2009, US$2.16 billion in 2010, and US$3.26 billion in 2011. It says the dividend policy was an entry condition agreed upon between former President Nestor Kirchner, Repsol, and the Peterson Group, which had put up little of its own cash and borrowed heavily from a consortium of banks and Repsol to pay for its shares. The YPF then agreed to pay 90 per cent of profits as dividends, so that the Peterson Group could repay its loans.[66]

The company also blames the country's energy policy with its aggressive subsidies, price controls and export taxes, for under-investment in exploration and production and over-consumption.[67] In July 2013, the government announced that it had agreed on a joint venture between YPF and US oil giant

62   *The New York Times*. 2012. 'Move on oil company draws praise in Argentina, where growth continues', 26 April. Available at: http://www.nytimes.com/2012/04/27/world/americas/ypf-nationalization-draws-praise-in-argentina.html?_r=0

63   *Mail Online*. 2012. 'Argentine President Plays to Evita Nickname as She Declares She Will Nationalise the Country's Largest Oil Company', 17 April.

64   Ibid.

65   BP Statistical Review. 2013. 'Argentina YPF Nationalization: Energy Crisis Provoked Government Expropriation of Repsol YPF', *Huffington Post*, 22 April, 2012. Available at: http://www.huffingtonpost.com/2012/04/22/repsol-argentina-ypf-nationalization_n_1444144.html [Accessed 14 November 2013].

66   *The Economist*. 2012. 'Fill'er up', 21 April. Available at http://www.economist.com/node/21553070 [Accessed 14 November 2013].

67   *The Huffington Post*. 2012. 'Argentina YPF Nationalization: Energy Crisis Provoked Government Expropriation of Repsol YPF', 22 April. Available at: http://www.huffingtonpost.com/2012/04/22/repsol-argentina-ypf-nationalization_n_1444144.html [Accessed on 14 November 2013]. *The Economist*. 2012. 'Cristina Scrapes The Barrel', 21 April. Available at: http://www.economist.com/node/21553031 [Accessed 14 November 2013].

Chevron, which would commit an initial US$1.24 billion to develop the Vaca Muerta (Dead Cow) field, which is estimated to hold 16 billion barrels of shale oil and 8.7 trillion cubic metres of shale gas. This field, which could result in Argentina having the world's fourth-largest reserves of shale oil and the second largest of shale gas, will require an estimated US$68 billion to US$89 billion to develop. YPF's new strategic plan provides an ambitious path to invest US$37.2 billion until 2017 to increase production and refining capacity.[68]

BOLIVIA

Bolivia is Latin America's poorest country with a GDP of just US$27.4 billion and a GDP per capita of US$5,099. It is one of the region's smallest economies. Bolivia had an era of modest economic growth from the post-war period to 1980. This was followed by a collapse of economic growth after a turn to the right and the introduction of neo-liberal economic policies after 1980. Between 1960 and 1980, Bolivia's GDP per capita grew by 2.3 per cent a year. Between 1981 and 2002, GDP per capita contracted by 0.3 per cent a year. Bolivia is a producer of oil (in small quantities), natural gas and metallic minerals. According to figures provided by the United States Geological Survey (USGS), preliminary estimates for 2011 showed that the output of these sectors was US$3.7 billion, equivalent to 15.5 per cent of the country's GDP.

The output of Bolivia's oil and gas sector was US$1.4 billion, equivalent to 5.9 per cent of GDP.[69] The sector also accounted for 30 per cent of government revenues and 45 per cent of total exports.[70] The output of the mining sector was US$2.3 billion, equivalent to 9.6 per cent of GDP. This included silver (US$1.4 billion), zinc (US$937 million), tin (US$520 million), gold (US$329 billion) and lead (US$242 million).[71] The extractive regime for oil and natural gas includes state ownership through Yacimentos Petroliferos Fiscales Bolivanos (YPFB), the national oil company (NOC), which has a small slice of the sector and an effective 50 per cent royalty for the private companies that dominate the industry. However, the country has not yet released a new mining code, which is expected to increase royalties from the present average of four per cent and announce plans to revitalise Corporacion Minera de Bolivia (Comibol), the

---

68 *The Economist.* 2013. 'Flogging a Dead Cow', 27 July. Available at: http://www.economist.com/news/americas/21582304-recently-nationalised-oil-company-agrees-big-foreign-investment-flogging-dead-cow [Accessed 14 November 2013].

69 S. Anderson. 2012. 'The Mineral Industry of Bolivia', United States Geological Survey. Available at: http://minerals.usgs.gov/minerals/pubs/country/sa.html [Accessed 14 November 2013].

70 US Energy Information Administration. 2012. Country Brief Bolivia. Available at: http://www.eia.gov/countries/cab.cfm?fips=BL [Accessed 14 November 2013].

71 S. Anderson. 2012. 'The Mineral Industry of Bolivia', United States Geological Survey. Available at: http://minerals.usgs.gov/minerals/pubs/country/sa.html [Accessed 14 November 2013].

state mining company.[72]

The natural gas sector has been a site of international interest and contest for much of the past century. In 1937, Bolivia became the first country in Latin America to nationalise its natural resources when it expropriated the assets of Standard Oil, which had been operating in the country since the 1920s, and gave them to the YPFB. In 1952, the country nationalised the tin sector and created a state-owned mining company, Comibol. Later, during the 1950s, the country opened its oil and gas sectors to foreign investment after pressure from the United States, which made the flow of aid conditional on the implementation of such a policy. While a number of foreign investors showed interest, the country granted concessions to Gulf Oil.

In 1969, Bolivia nationalised Gulf Oil and gave its assets to YPFB. During the mid-1980s, the country entered another privatisation cycle as it sought to gain approval from international lending agencies led by the International Monetary Fund (IMF). Under the Plan de Todos, the government announced plans to privatise five of its largest public industries: electricity generation and distribution, telecommunications, airlines, railways, and oil and gas extraction and distribution. The state auctioned off the majority of shares in these industries, and reallocated the remaining shares to the state pension system and former employees. The terms of the IMF agreement excluded the state from productive enterprises and direct financial investment. Its role was limited to creating the conditions for markets to operate and making investments in areas such as primary education and healthcare.[73]

A decade of intense neoliberal policymaking from 1995 to 2005 resulted in the dismantling of YPBF[74] and a stripping of the capacities of what had been the country's most important company: a vertically-integrated monopoly which had controlled nearly all of Bolivia's oil and gas sector.[75] Between 1985 and 1996, YPFB's revenues constituted the primary source of income for the state. For the six years prior to its privatisation in 1996, YPBF transferred an annual average of US$300 million to the treasury. In 1996, YPBF had an income of US$562.8 million, of which US$279.6 million (50 per cent of its income) was

72 *The Globe and Mail.* 2011. 'Bolivia Plans to Hike Royalties', 1 September. Available at: http://www.theglobeandmail.com report-on-business/international-business/latin-american-business/bolivia-plans-to-hike-mining-royalties/article1356627/ [Accessed November 2013].

73 B. Kaup. 2010. 'A Neoliberal Nationalisation: The Constraints on Natural Gas Led Development in Bolivia', *Latin American Perspectives* 37: 3: 123–128. Available at: http://wmpeople.wm.edu/site/page/bzkaup/publications [Accessed November 2013].

74 B. Kohl and L. Farthing. 2012. 'Material Constraints to Popular Imaginaries: The Extractive Economy and Resource Nationalism in Bolivia', *Political Geography Volume 31, Issue 4,* May, pp. 225–235. Available at: http://www.sciencedirect.com/science/article/pii/S0962629812000212 [Accessed November 2013].

75 B. Kaup. 2010. 'A Neoliberal Nationalisation: The Constraints on Natural Gas Led Development in Bolivia', *Latin American Perspectives* 37: 3: 123–128. Available at: http://wmpeople.wm.edu/site/page/bzkaup/publications [Accessed November 2013].

transferred to the treasury.[76] The fire sale that followed changed the face of the industry and constrained subsequent attempts to re-assert control over oil and gas production and transform it into an engine of development.

Between 1994 and 1996, the government divided YPFB into three companies (Chaco, Andina, and Transredes) and auctioned 50 per cent of each to the highest bidder. The remaining 50 per cent was transferred to a so-called capitalisation fund, whose dividends were invested and administered as pension funds for all Bolivians aged 21 by 31 December 1995.[77] Chaco and Andina were in the upstream industry, while Transredes took over YPBF's pipelines. The World Bank had valued the companies at US$961 million but they were eventually sold for US$835 million. Suprisingly, the government never saw this money. The winning bidders had committed to reinvesting the money in the companies over seven years. The next step was to reduce the government take and further subsidise the bidders. Before privatisation, private companies working with YPBF were subject to a 50 per cent tax on the value of production. The government and the IMF introduced a new system. There was a 50 per cent royalty for 'existing reserves' and an 18 per cent royalty for 'new reserves'. Only three per cent of reserves were classified as 'existing'. Effectively, there was a massive drop in the royalty rate. To compensate government for the loss of revenue, the IMF went for consumers, who were now required to pay a new sales tax when buying fuel or airline and bus tickets.

An analysis of the costs and benefits of this arrangement between 1999 and 2004 showed that the revenue foregone by the government was US$2.2 billion, which included the US$835 million exemption from paying for the assets they received from YPBF given to the winning bidders and another US$839 million given to the same companies due to the effective reduction of royalty payments from 50 to 18 per cent. The benefits were almost US$1.4 billion including royalties and taxes (US$1.2 billion) and dividends to the capitalisation fund (US$130 million). In addition, investment in the industry increased to an annual average of US$374 million during the nine years after privatisation (1996 to 2005) compared with US$102 million a year during the six years before privatisation (1990 to 2006). By 2004, industry had a turnover of almost US$1.2 billion compared with US$291 million in 1999.[78]

As a result, proven and probable natural gas and oil reserves soared. While

---

76 C. McGuigan. 2007. 'The Benefits of FDI: Is Foreign Investment in Bolivia's Oil and Gas Delivering?' Christian Aid and the Centre for Labour and Agrarian Development Research. Available at: http://www.christianaid.org.uk/images/ca-oil-gas-bolivia.pdf [Accessed November 2013].

77 Ibid.

78 C. McGuigan. 2007. 'The Benefits of FDI: Is Foreign Investment in Bolivia's Oil and Gas Delivering?' Christian Aid and the Centre for Labour and Agrarian Development Research. Available at: http://www.christianaid.org.uk/images/ca-oil-gas-bolivia.pdf [Accessed November 2013].

investment and extraction increased, the majority of Bolivians failed to see the benefits. A plan to export natural gas to the United States via Chile became a focal point for social movement protests, which led to the fall of the then president. Bolivians voted in a referendum to nationalise the hydrocarbon sector, refund YPFB and increase tax and royalty rates. The new president resigned due to popular pressure in June 2005 after failing to implement the reforms. Six months later, Bolivia elected a new president, Evo Morales, who took office in January 2006, promising to start the country's third cycle of nationalisation.[79] On May Day the same year, President Morales sent troops to take control of at least 56 fields. He went to the large San Alberto field operated by Petrobrás, the Brazilian NOC, and Repsol-YPF of Spain, the two largest companies, which controlled 74 per cent of country's gas reserves, and announced that *el gas es nuestro* – the gas is ours.

After brinkmanship from both sides, the government and the private companies reached an agreement which has been described as 'nationalisation without expropriation.'[80] According to one account: 'Morales sent the military to oil and gas sites but seized no foreign assets, unfurled Bolivia's national flag but replaced no foreign companies. Companies' operations and autonomy went largely unhindered.'[81] The key elements of the agreement were a return to the situation before privatisation. The government granted formal ownership of oil and gas reserves to YFPB.[82] It renegotiated supply contracts with Brazil and Argentina, the country's main export customers, resulting in a large increase in revenues.[83] The government also abolished the differentiation between existing and new reserves. All reserves became subject to the 18 per cent royalty. But to achieve parity with the pre-privatisation royalty rate, Bolivia introduced a new 32 per cent direct tax (the Impuesto Directo en los Hidrocarburos or IDH) on the value of production, which operates like a royalty but is formulated as a tax because the contracts with foreign investors did not allow the government to change royalty payments.

However, the tax does not all flow to national government. Given the structure of the Bolivian law, the IDH proceeds must be distributed to departments (provinces where the oil and gas is produced), municipalities, universities, and indigenous groups, and be used primarily for education, roads and healthcare.[84]

---

79   B. Kaup. 2010. 'Bolivia's Nationalised Natural Gas: Social and Economic Stability Under Morales', London School of Economic Ideas Centre, Latin America Energy Diplomacy Strategy Report. Available at: http://www.lse.ac.uk/IDEAS/publications/reports/pdf/SU005/kaup.pdf [Accessed November 2013].

80   Ibid.

81   US Energy Information Administration. 2012. Country Brief Bolivia. Available at: http://www.eia.gov/countries/cab.cfm?fips=BL

82   Ibid.

83   B. Kaup. 2010. 'A Neoliberal Nationalisation: The Constraints on Natural Gas Led Development in Bolivia', *Latin American Perspectives* 37: 3: 123–128. Available at: http://wmpeople.wm.edu/site/page/bzkaup/publications [Accessed November 2013].

84   C. McGuigan. 2007. 'The Benefits of FDI: Is Foreign Investment in Bolivia's Oil and Gas Delivering?' Christian Aid and the Centre for Labour and Agrarian Development Research. Available at: http://www.christianaid.org.uk/images/ca-oil-gas-bolivia.pdf [Accessed November 2013].

As a result, only 25 per cent accrues to the national government. Another 25 per cent accrues to YPFB, and the remaining half goes to sub-national structures.[85] Finally, the new policy allowed the emaciated YPFB to participate in the whole supply of an oil and gas industry chain.[86] To start the process, government negotiated with the owners of the previously privatised operations of YPFB to regain control. In May 2008, the government paid US$48 million to take control of Chaco, Andina, Transredes and CLHB, an oil-tanking firm.[87] However, at the time of the so-called nationalisation, Chaco and Andina extracted only 6.3 per cent of Bolivia's national gas.[88]

Today, international oil companies (IOCs) still extract the majority of the country's natural gas and minerals, although the share going to the state has changed dramatically. Income from oil and gas, which now accounts for half of state revenue, increased from US$173 million in 2002 to more than US$2.2 billion in 2011.[89] Hydrocarbon revenues increased from 5.6 per cent of GDP in 2004 to a high of 25.7 per cent in 2009. Public investment increased from 6.3 per cent of GDP in 2005 to 10.5 per cent of GDP in 2009.[90] As a result, capital formation increased from 11 per cent of GDP in 2004 to 19.6 per cent of GDP in 2011.[91] The government also used fiscal policy effectively to counter the impact of the global financial crisis (GFC). The government's fiscal position went from a surplus of five per cent of GDP in the first quarter of 2008 to a deficit of 0.7 per cent of GDP in the first quarter of 2009, a huge shift of nearly six per cent of GDP. This was probably the most important policy move that helped Bolivia avoid the worst effects of the GFC. The Bolivian economy grew by 3.4 per cent in 2009,[92] and by 4.8 per cent a year between 2006 and 2012. By comparison, real GDP per capita declined between 1950 and 2000. There has not been similar success in the case of non-fuel minerals. According to Kohl

85   Weisbrot and Sandoval. 2008. 'The Distribution of Bolivia's Most Important Natural Resources and the Autonomy Conflicts', Centre for Economic Policy Research. Available at: http://www.cepr.net/index.php/publications/reports/the-distribution-of-bolivias-most-important-natural-resources-and-the-autonomy-conflicts [Accessed November 2013].

86   C. McGuigan. 2007. 'The Benefits of FDI: Is Foreign Investment in Bolivia's Oil and Gas Delivering?' Christian Aid and the Centre for Labour and Agrarian Development Research. Available at: http://www.christianaid.org.uk/images/ca-oil-gas-bolivia.pdf [Accessed November 2013].

87   BILLION Americas. 2008. 'Government Takes Over Transredes, Andina, Chaco and CLHB', 2 May. Available at: http://www.billionamericas.com/news/privatization/Government_takes_over_Transredes,_Andina,_Chaco,_CLHB [Accessed November 2013].

88   B. Kaup. 2010. 'Bolivia's Nationalised Natural Gas: Social and Economic Stability Under Morales', London School of Economic Ideas Centre, Latin America Energy Diplomacy Strategy Report. Available at: http://www.lse.ac.uk/IDEAS/publications/reports/pdf/SU005/kaup.pdf [Accessed November 2013].

89   B. Kohl and L. Farthing. 2012. 'Material Constraints to Popular Imagineries: The Extractive Economy and Resource Nationalism in Bolivia', *Political Geography Volume 31, Issue 4*, May, pp. 225–235. Available at: http://www.sciencedirect.com/science/article/pii/S0962629812000212 [Accessed November 2013].

90   Weisbrot, Ray and Johnston. 2009. 'Bolivia: The Economy During the Morales Administration', Centre for Economic Policy Research. Available at: http://www.cepr.net/index.php/publications/reports/bolivian-economy-during-morales-administration/ [Accessed January 2014].

91   International Monetary Fund (IMF) World Economic Outlook Database. Available at: http://www.imf.org/external/pubs/ft/weo/2013/02/weodata/weoselgr.aspx [Accessed January 2014].

92   Weisbrot, Ray and Johnston. 2009. 'Bolivia: The Economy During the Morales Administration', Centre for Economic Policy Research. Available at: http://www.cepr.net/index.php/publications/reports/bolivian-economy-during-morales-administration/ [Accessed January 2014].

and Farthing (2012), since assuming office in 2006, the ruling Movement for Socialism (MAS) has repeatedly seen its efforts to increase mining royalties and revenues thwarted by the powerful cooperative miners' federation.[93] As a result, there have been numerous delays in releasing a new mining code.

BRAZIL

Brazil is by far the largest economy in South America, and the seventh largest in the world, with a GDP of US$2.4 trillion, equivalent to 56 per cent of the region's total.[94] In line with most countries in the region, Brazil had an era of successful economic growth from the post-war period to 1980. This was followed by a collapse of economic growth after a turn to the right and the introduction of neo-liberal economic policies after 1980. Between 1960 and 1980, Brazil's GDP per capita grew by 4.6 per cent a year.[95] Between 1981 and 2002, GDP per capita grew by just 0.1 per cent a year. Cumulatively, GDP per capita grew by 123 per cent between 1960 and 1980, and by eight per cent between 1980 and 2000. If Brazil had simply continued to grow at its pre-1980 rate, which was much lower than South Korea's and Taiwan's growth over the same period, the country would have had European living standards a decade ago.[96]

Today, Brazil is a major producer of oil, gas and minerals (mostly iron ore) with a national champion in each sector. These are Petroleo Brasileiro (Petrobrás), the national oil company (NOC) with revenues of US$144 billion and Vale, the global mining company, with revenues of US$47 billion. In 2010, the two sectors accounted for 29 per cent of the country's total exports, with oil and gas accounting for 9.8 per cent and minerals accounting for 19 per cent.[97] However, Brazil has a relatively low ratio of exports to GDP of about 13 per cent.[98] As a result, the combined contribution of the country's extractive industries to GDP was just above three per cent in 2010. This also reflects the large and diversified nature of the country's economy. The contribution to the employment total was a mere 300,000 jobs in 2009, less than one per cent

93 B. Kohl and L. Farthing. 2012. 'Material Constraints to Popular Imagineries: The Extractive Economy and Resource Nationalism in Bolivia', *Political Geography Volume 31, Issue 4*, May, pp. 225–235. Available at: http://www.sciencedirect.com/science/article/pii/S0962629812000212 [Accessed November 2013].

94 International Monetary Fund. 2013. 'Regional Economic Outlook: Western Hemisphere'. Available at: http://www.imf.org/external/pubs/ft/reo/2013/whd/eng/wreo0513.htm [Accessed November 2013].

95 A. Solimano and R. Soto. 2005. 'Economic Growth in Latin America in the Late 20th Century: Evidence and Interpretation', Economic Commission for Latin America and the Caribbean (Cepal). Available at: http://www.cepal.org/publicaciones/xml/5/21325/lcl2236i.pdf[Accessed November 2013].

96 M. Weisbrot and L. Sandoval. 2006. 'Brazil's Presidential Election: Background on Economic Issues', Centre for Economic Policy and Research. Available at: http://www.cepr.net/documents/Brazil_2006_09_22.pdf [Accessed January 2014].

97 International Council on Mining and Metals. 2012. 'The Role of Mining in National Economies'. Available at: http://www.icmm.com/the-role-of-mining-in-national-economies [Accessed November 2013].

98 Information obtained from: http://www.quandl.com/economics/exports-as-share-of-gdp-all-countries [Accessed January 2014].

of the country's labour force, with mining accounting for 232,000 jobs. This reflects the highly capital-intensive nature of these extractive industries.[99]

Brazil's extractive regime is aggressive in the oil and gas industry where there is a relatively high level of state ownership, and docile in the mining industry where there is limited state ownership and comparatively low royalties. Petrobrás, in which the government owns 48 per cent of ordinary, and 64 per cent of voting, shares,[100] was established in 1953 under the Presidency of Getulio Vargas with a monopoly of oil production and importing. When it started operations in 1954, it produced just 2,700 barrels per day (bpd). As discoveries were made, production increased to 181,000 bpd in 1980; 653,000 bpd in 1990; 1,271,000 bpd in 2000; and 1,980,000 in 2012.[101] In 1997, the government opened the sector to competition. Since then, many International Oil Companies (IOC) have entered the market. In August 2003, Shell became the first IOC to start production. Others have followed, including Chevron, BP, Andarko, Statoil, Repsol, and Sinopec.[102] Since 1999, ANP, the Brazilian National Agency of Petroleum, Natural Gas and Biofuels, the industry regulator, has had 12 rounds of licensing and the first one for the new pre-salt production sharing contracts (PSCs).[103] Up to 2012, 78 companies acquired exploration and production licences, out of which 53, including Petrobrás, have started operations.

According to the law, concession agreements must provide for the following government takes: a signature bonus, royalties, special participation and payment for occupation of an area. The minimum signature bonus is specified in the bid invitation. Royalties are set at a maximum of 10 per cent of sales revenue, but may be reduced to a minimum of five per cent depending on a number of factors, including geological risks and production forecasts. Special participation is a tax of between 10 per cent and 40 per cent for operators of high volume or profit margin fields. The bid document also specifies a landowner royalty, calculated per square metre, payable for occupation of an area. In evaluating a bid, ANP must take into account the following criteria: the signature bonus (40 per cent weighting), the minimum work programme (40 per cent) and local content (20 per cent). Each bidding round specifies a

99   International Council on Mining and Metals. 2013. 'The Mining Sector in Brazil: Building Sustainable institutions for Sustainable Development'. Available at: http://www.google.co.za/url?sa=t&rct=j&q=&esrc=s&source=web&cd=7&cad=rja&ved=0CGQQFjAG&url=http%3A%2F%2Fwww.icmm.com%2Fdocument%2F5423&ei=IhHiUuuUDZOShgfGpoD4AQ&usg=AFQjCNFQ-0bVwELqHN4ln7Fp6vZZ1rZZaA&bvm=bv.59930103,d.bGQ [Accessed January 2014].

100 Petrobrás. 2013. 'Petrobrás at a Glance', January. Presentation available at: http://investidorpetrobras.com.br/en/home.htm [Accessed November 2013].

101 Petrobras Fact Sheet. Available at: http://www.investidorpetrobras.com.br/en/investor-s-center/fact-sheet.htm [Accessed November 2013].

102 US Energy Information Administration. 2013. Country Brief Brazil. Available at: http://www.eia.gov/countries/cab.cfm?fips=BR.

103 Magda Chambriard. 2013. 'Opportunities for Investors in the Brazilian Oil and Gas Industry and 1st Pre-Salt Round', ANP Presentation available at: http://www.brazil.org.uk/commercial/anproadshow_files/anproadshow2013.pdf [Accessed November 2013].

minimum local content percentage.[104]

Despite massive foreign interest in the sector, Petrobras still produces 96 per cent of the country's oil.[105] In 2012, Petrobrás, which has listings on the Brazilian and New York Stock Exchanges and operations in 24 countries, had sales of US$144 billion and a market capitalisation of US$127 billion. The company is expected to double in size by 2020 on the back of recent discoveries of pre-salt oil, so called because the fields are located 300km offshore, five to seven kilometres below the seabed under a 2km layer of salt and another 2km layer of rock. The new finds have doubled the country's reserves to 30 billion barrels. Production will more than double to 5.7 million bpd by 2020. As a result, Petrobrás has announced that it will invest US$237 billion between 2013 and 2017,[106] the world's biggest capital expenditure programme according to the *Financial Times*. According to some estimates, there could be at least 50 billion barrels of pre-salt deposits, which would require US$1,000 billion of investments over 10 years – the largest private sector investment programme in the history of mankind, the newspaper says.[107]

The government has introduced a new regulatory framework for the pre-salt reserves, which includes: the establishment of a pre-salt agency to administer production and trading contracts; the capitalisation of Petrobrás by granting it 5 billion barrels of unlicensed pre-salt in exchange for a higher shareholding; the establishment of a new development fund to manage government revenues from the new industry; and the introduction of a new production sharing agreement (PSA) system. In contrast to the concessions for non-pre-salt, Petrobrás will be the sole operator of each PSA and hold a minimum 30 per cent share in all projects. The government has also introduced 65 per cent local content requirements for the industry.[108]

In 2010, Brazil had the world's third largest mining sector in terms of production value after China and Australia. Between 2000 and 2010, mining production increased by 507 per cent, most of which related to an increase in world iron ore prices and a doubling of production from 157 million tonnes

104 Baker & McKenzie. 2013. 'Latin America', *Oil & Gas Handbook*. Available at: http://www.bakermckenzie.com/files/Uploads/
     Documents/Global%20EMI/bk_la_oilgas_12.pdf [Accessed November 2013].
     KPMG. 2011. *A Guide to Brazilian Oil & Gas Taxation*. Available at: https://www.kpmg.com/global/en/issuesandinsights/
     articlespublications/pages/brazilian-oil-gas-taxation.aspx [Accessed November 2013].
105 Petrobras. 2013. 'Petrobrás at a Glance', September. Presentation available at: http://investidorpetrobras.com.br/en/presentations/
     petrobras-at-a-glance.htm [Accessed November 2013].
106 Ibid.
107 *Financial Times*. 2011. 'Brazil: Platform for Growth', 15 March. Available at: http://www.ft.com/intl/cms/s/0/fa11320c-4f48-11e0-
     9038-00144feab49a.html?siteedition=uk#axzz2I9UrtWNj [Accessed November 2013].
108 US Energy Information Administration. Country Brief Brazil. Available at: http://www.eia.gov/countries/cab.cfm?fips=BR [Accessed
     November 2013].

in 2000 to 310 million tonnes in 2010.[109] In 2012, the country's mineral production was US$51 billion. It had mineral exports of US$38.7 billion, with iron ore accounting for US$31 billion or 80 per cent of the total. Brazil has the world's second largest iron ore reserves: 28 billion tonnes, equivalent to 16.1 per cent of the global reserves of 180 billion tonnes. In 2011, Brazil, with output of 391.1 million tonnes, was the world's third largest producer of iron ore after China and Australia. Vale produced 84.5 per cent of the country's iron ore. Other large producers included Samarco (6.29 per cent) and CSN (5.45 per cent). In 2012, the country also exported large amounts of gold (US$2.3 billion), Niobium (US$1.8 billion) and Copper (US$1.5 billion).[110]

Vale was established by the Brazilian government in 1942 under the name Companhia Vale do Rio Doce (CVRD), with a mandate to mine, trade, transport and export iron and operate a railroad which carried iron ore and agricultural products. The company was listed on the Rio De Janeiro Stock Exchange in 1943. In 1997, the Brazilian government privatised the company. In 1998, the company changed its name to Vale. Today, Vale, with operations in 30 countries, is the world's largest producer of iron ore and the second largest producer of nickel.

In 2012, Vale had revenues of US$46.7 billion, of which 69 per cent was from iron ore and pellets. The largest shareholder, with a 33.7 per cent stake, is Valepar, a special-purpose vehicle comprising Brazilian steelmakers, pension funds, investment companies and foreign investors who bought the government shares during the privatisation. There is a free float of 61.2 per cent of the shares, which is owned by various institutional and retail investors. The government of Brazil, through BILLIONDES, the state-owned development bank, owns 5.1 per cent of the shares and 12 'golden shares', which give it the right to veto certain important decisions, including changes to the name, location of the head office, and the purpose of the business and disposals.[111]

109   International Council on Mining and Metals. 2012. 'The Role of Mining in National Economies'. Available at: http://www.icmm. com/the-role-of-mining-in-national-economies [Accessed November 2013].
International Council on Mining and Metals. 2013. 'The Mining Sector in Brazil: Building Sustainable Institutions for Sustainable Development'. Available at: http://www.google.co.za/ url?sa=t&rct=j&q=&esrc=s&source=web&cd=7&cad=rja&ved=0CGQQFjAG&url=http%3A%2F%2Fwww.icmm.com%2Fdocu ment%2F5423&ei=IhHiUuuUDZOShgfGpoD4AQ&usg=AFQjCNFQ-0bVwELqHN4ln7Fp6vZZ1rZZaA&bvm=bv.59930103,d.bGQ [Accessed January 2014].

110   IBRAM. 2012. *Information and Analyses of the Brazilian Mineral Economy, 7th edition*, December. Available at: http://www.ibram. org.br/sites/1400/1457/00000365.pdf [Accessed November 2012].
Gurmendi. 2013. 'The Mineral Industry of Brazil in 2011', *Minerals Yearbook*. Brazil: United States Geological Survey. Available at: http://minerals.usgs.gov/minerals/pubs/country/2011/myb3-2011-br.pdf [Accessed November 2013].

111   Vale Fact Sheet. Available at: http://www.vale.com/EN/investors/company/fact-sheet/Pages/default.aspx [Accessed November 2013]. Vale Shareholders Structure Chart. Available at: http://assets.vale.com/docs/Documents/en/investors/Company/ shareholding-structure/Shareholder_structure_i.pdf [Accessed November 2013]. Vale 2012 Annual Report. Available at: http:// www.vale.com/EN/investors/Quarterly-results-Reports/20F/20FDocs/20F_2012_i.pdf [Accessed November 2013].

In 2012, Brazil collected mining royalties of about US$800 million, equivalent to a mere 1.6 per cent of the industry's revenues of US$51 billion. Brazil's royalties on net revenues are: three per cent for aluminium ore, manganese, salt-gem and potassium; two per cent for iron, fertiliser and coal; one per cent for gold; and 0.2 per cent for precious stones, cuttable coloured stones, carbonate and noble metals. The revenues are distributed between federal government (12 per cent), the state where the mineral is produced (23 per cent), and the producing municipality (65 per cent). The government shares its contribution with the National Department of Mineral Production (9.8 per cent), a technology innovation fund (two per cent) and an environmental agency (0.2 per cent).[112] The government has released a new draft mining code that could result in the establishment of a National Mining Agency, a National Council for Mineral Policy, and an increase in maximum royalties to four per cent from two per cent. This would increase the total royalty take from US$800 million to close to US$2 billion. According to *The Economist*, this would bring Brazil's light taxes on mineral wealth closer to those levied in other countries, for example Australia, which charges up to 12 per cent.[113]

CHILE

Chile's population of 17.4 million, with a GDP per capita of US$18,419 in 2012, has the highest standard of living in Latin America. From 1938 to 1973, Chile pursued state-led economic development policies, including import substitution. The government protected domestic producers and its agencies became the most important entrepreneurs in the economy, initiating ventures in numerous industries. Swathes of the industrial sector sprung up under government entrepreneurship: steel, petroleum extraction and processing, sugar, vertically integrated electricity generation and distribution, and telecommunications.[114] Between 1971 and 1973, there was a brief period of socialism under President Salvador Allende, who nationalised the country's copper industry and many other large companies.

After a military coup led by General Augusto Pinochet in 1973, the country went to the other extreme, embracing the free-market fundamentalism of the 'Chicago Boys', the dictator's economic advisers who had studied under Milton Friedman, the doyen of free-market capitalism, at the University of Chicago. Chile became the world's first laboratory for neo-liberal policies that were

112 IBRAM. 2012. *Information and Analyses of the Brazilian Mineral Economy,* 7th edition, December. Available at: http://www.ibram. org.br/sites/1400/1457/00000365.pdf [Accessed November 2012].

113 *The Economist.* 2013. 'Time to Dig Deep', 22 June. Available at: http://www.economist.com/news/americas/21579872-long-awaited-bill-ends-uncertainty-will-hit-mining-companies-profits-time-dig-deep [Accessed November 2013].

114 M. Agosin, C. Larraín and N. Grau. 2010. 'Industrial Policy In Chile', Inter-American Development Bank Working Paper Series No. IDB-WP-170. Available at: http://www.iadb.org/res/publications/pubfiles/pubIDB-WP-170.pdf [Accessed November 2013].

being developed in Chicago. The 'shock therapy' included 400 privatisations that returned nationalised companies (excluding the national copper company) to their previous owners. After the return to democracy in 1990, the country was led by centre-left coalitions which continued Pinochet's economic policies, albeit with a human face, with higher levels of social spending. With continued privatisation, inflation targeting, budget surpluses and low levels of public debt, Chile became a poster child for the Washington consensus. The country's GDP growth averaged 7.1 per cent a year between 1990 and 1997 and then slowed down to 2.3 per cent a year between 1997 and 2003. The period of fast growth was associated with large private sector investments in the country's copper industry.

Copper has been used in Chile since ancient times. Indigenous people worked the red metal into tools, utensils and even alloys with other metals that were traded. During the colonial period, until 1810, the Spanish were more interested in gold. Between 1820 and 1900 the country produced 2 million tonnes. But large-scale copper mining started in 1904 when the American Braden Copper Company began operations at the El Teniente mine.[115] State influence over the copper industry increased gradually. The Chilean state used to receive very little return from copper until the signing of the Washington Agreement with the US government in 1951, which gave Chile control of 20 per cent of production. In 1955, several laws were passed in order to guarantee minimum revenue for the Chilean state and to promote the development of the industry. The Copper department was created to oversee the industry.[116]

In 1966, the 'Chileanisation of Copper' law created a framework for joint ventures between the Chilean state and foreign mining companies. It set a minimum state interest of 25 per cent for large-scale copper mining. In 1967, the El Teniente, Chuquicamata and Salvador mines became joint ventures with the state holding 51 per cent. In the case of Exotica and Andina, the state acquired 25 per cent. In 1971, Allende took the process further and nationalised the industry. Large-scale mining became wholly owned by the Chilean state. In order to manage these resources, state-owned general par trillionerships were created with the Copper Corporation (95 per cent) and Empressa Nacional de Mineira (five per cent). However, in 1976, Pinochet's government created Corporación Nacional del Cobre de Chile (CODELCO), which took over the mining deposits and replaced the state general par trillionerships. The mines at Chuquicamata, Exótica, El Teniente, Salvador and Andina were grouped together in one company.[117]

---

115 *CODELCO Annual Report 2011.* Available at: http://www.codelco.com/flipbook/memorias/memoria2011/en/history.html [Accessed November 2013].

116 Ibid.

117 Ibid.

Pinochet's CODELCO represents a case study of successful nationalisation, a positive counterfactual argument put forward by Zambia against state ownership. In 1970, Zambia produced 819,000 tonnes compared with 692,000 tonnes in Chile. Zambia bought only 51 per cent of Anglo American's operations in 1969.[118] It should have succeeded because it remained in a joint venture with an experienced miner. On the other hand, Chile took over 100 per cent of the industry in 1973. It has been argued that Zambia suffered because of falling copper prices, but Chile shows that this was not the whole story. The major reason for the decline was the uninterrupted decline in copper production from 825,000 tonnes in 1969 to 250,000 tonnes in 2000.[119] Chile returned to democracy in 1990 and Zambians voted the following year. The two countries have much in common. But the paths they took are miles apart.

Today, Chile is the world's largest producer of copper. In 2012, the country produced 5,433.9 million tonnes of copper, equivalent to 31.8 per cent of the world's total production, according to Comisíon Chilena del Cobre (COCHILCO), the country's copper commission. During the same year, copper mining contributed 10.8 per cent to the country's GDP and employed 54,538 people. Other mining activities generated 1.2 per cent of GDP. In 2012, the country had copper exports of US$42.3 billion, equivalent to 89 per cent of total mining exports. Other important mining exports included gold (US$1.7 billion), molybdenum (US$1.7 billion), iron ore (US$1.3 billion) and silver (US$623 million). The country's extractive regime includes state-owned CODELCO, which is the world's largest producer, and various royalties and taxes paid by multinational mining companies. Major private sector producers include: Escondida, the world's largest copper mine owned by BHP Billiton, and Rio Tinto (with production of 1.1 million tonnes); Los Pelambres (417,700 tonnes) and Anglo American Sur (416,600 tonnes).[120] In January 2006, Chile started implementing a new royalty system. The royalty tax is between 0.5 per cent and five per cent of production. The five per cent rate applies to production of more than 50,000 tonnes. Therefore, large companies pay five per cent.[121]

In 2012, CODELCO had sales of US$15.9 billion and made a pre-tax profit of US$7.5 billion. It produced 1,646.5 million tonnes, equivalent to 9.6 per

---

118 P. Meller, A. Simpasa, B. Lara and G. Valdés. 2011. 'Role of Copper in the Chilean and Zambian Economies: Main Economic and Policy Issues', Global Development Network Working Paper Series. Available at: http://www.gdn.int/admin/uploads/editor/files/WP43_Chile_Zambia_Copper.pdf [Accessed November 2013].

119 H. Van der Heijden. 2001. 'Zambian Policy-Making and the Donor Community in the 1990s', UNU-WIDER. Available at: http://www.wider.unu.edu/publications/search/en_GB/browse-by-jel-code/?sortBy=1&sortOrder=desc&start_at=1&JEL=Q-Agricultural and Natural Resource Economics;Environmental and Ecological Economics [Accessed November 2013].

120 Comision Chilena del Cobre. 2013. *Yearbook: Copper and Other Mineral Statistics 1993–2012.* Available at: http://www.cochilco.cl/descargas/estadisticas/anuarios/AE2013web.pdf [Accessed November 2013].

121 P. Meller, A. Simpasa, B. Lara and G. Valdés. 2011. 'Role of Copper in the Chilean and Zambian Economies: Main Economic and Policy Issues', Global Development Network Working Paper Series. Available at: http://www.gdn.int/admin/uploads/editor/files/WP43_Chile_Zambia_Copper.pdf [Accessed November 2013].

cent of world production and 30.3 per cent of Chilean output. CODELCO's share of Chilean copper production reduced steadily from 75 per cent in 1990[122] to 30.3 per cent in 2012 as multinational mining companies entered the industry.[123] The entry of multinationals was associated with a sharp increase in production to almost 4.9 million tonnes in 2003 from 1.6 million tonnes in 1990. Between 1991 and 2003, mining multinationals invested US$15.5 billion in the industry.[124]

In fact, the country's copper industry has performed admirably over a longer period. Maxwell (2004) says that, even though worldwide demand and production of copper rose at an annual rate of three per cent from 1960 to 2001, copper prices in real dollar terms fell by two per cent a year over the same period. Unless offset by favourable exchange rate movements, producers have had to increase output on average by this amount to generate the same revenue stream. In this challenging environment, Chilean mine production soared by almost 600 per cent from 692,000 tonnes in 1970 to 4.7 million tonnes in 2001 as the country increased its share of world copper production from 10 to 34 per cent. However, the value of production only doubled over the period, due to copper prices and the exchange rate.[125] These figures suggest that the Chilean public-private model has allowed it to get the best of both worlds: using a state company to extract rents while attracting private investment.

A closer look at the model shows the effectiveness of state ownership in extracting rents. A comparison of the government take from public and private producers, after the introduction of a new royalty regime in 2006, shows that CODELCO, with half the production of the top 10 private producers, generated more tax revenues. CODELCO's payments to government are: the normal corporate tax rate of 17 per cent, which applies to all companies; an additional 40 per cent that is payable by all public entities; and 10 per cent of export revenues which is paid to the armed forces. Between 2006 and 2012, CODELCO paid US$42.5 billion to the government.[126] But the top 10 copper mining companies, which accounted for 63 per cent of national production, paid US$29.2 billion over the same period. In 2012, the combined tax contribution was US$8.4 billion (with 50 per cent from CODELCO),

122 *The Economist.* 2010. 'Reviving Codelco', 21 October. Available at: http://www.economist.com/node/17311933 [Accessed November 2013].

123 Comision Chilena del Cobre. 2013. *Yearbook: Copper and Other Mineral Statistics 1993–2012.* Available at: http://www.cochilco. cl/descargas/estadisticas/anuarios/AE2013web.pdf [Accessed November 2013].

124 International Council on Mining and Metals. 2010. 'Chile: The Challenges of Mineral Wealth: Using Resource Endowments to Foster Sustainable Development'. Available at: https://www.google.co.za/?gws_rd=cr&ei=ITSgUvOTLtDUsgb8nYDYAg# [Accessed November 2013].

125 P. Maxwell. 2004. 'Chile's Recent Copper-Driven Prosperity: Does it Provide Lessons For Other Mineral-Rich Developing Countries?' *Minerals and Energy – Raw Materials Report,* 19: 1, 16–31.

126 Comision Chilena del Cobre. 2013. *Yearbook: Copper and Other Mineral Statistics 1993–2012.* Available at: http://www.cochilco. cl/descargas/estadisticas/anuarios/AE2013web.pdf [Accessed November 2013].

equivalent to 14.2 per cent of total government revenues. Finally, between 2003 and 2012, the top 10 mining companies invested US$20.4 billion in the industry while CODELCO invested US$18.4 billion.[127] The state mining company's production has remained at about 1.6 million tonnes for a decade. The company has now announced a US$27 billion investment plan over the next six years to increase production to more than 2 million tonnes.[128]

In 1985, Chile established a Copper Stabilisation Fund (CSF) that started operations two years later. The fund had a mandate to accumulate part of CODELCO's income when the copper price is above a certain reference price. In 2006, the government passed the Fiscal Responsibility Law (FRL) that created two funds to manage increased revenues from mining royalty payments and CODELCO. The FRL extends the commitment of the government to a structural fiscal surplus rule that was established in 2000 to help insulate the economy from fluctuations in mineral commodity prices. During a boom, this rule allows the government to spend only a portion of the surplus revenue that is considered permanent and to save the transitory portion. As part of the FRL, a panel of six members was selected to form a council to advise the minister of finance on investment guidelines for the funds and to determine the permanent and transitory portions of revenue.

The first fund was called the Economic and Social Stabilisation Fund (ESSF), which was established in 2006 with an initial investment of US$6 billion, mostly from the closure of the old CSF. The second fund is called the Pension Reserve Fund and was established with US$600 million. At the end of 2011, the two funds had assets of US$13.2 billion and US$4.4 billion respectively.[129] The fund had accumulated more than US$20 billion – more than 15 per cent of GDP – just before the global financial crisis (GFC) of 2008. This became controversial. According to *The Wall Street Journal*, protestors barged into a presentation by Andres Velasco carrying his effigy and shouting: 'The copper money is for the poor people.' Soon afterwards, world copper prices plummeted by more than 50 per cent at the onset of the GFC. In January 2009, Chile announced a US$4 billion fiscal stimulus financed by withdrawals from the ESSF. It included a US$1 billion capitalisation of CODELCO and an injection of US$500 million into state-owned Banco Estado.[130]

127 Comision Chilena del Cobre. 2013. *Yearbook: Copper and Other Mineral Statistics 1993–2012*. Available at: http://www.cochilco.cl/descargas/estadisticas/anuarios/AE2013web.pdf [Accessed November 2013].

128 *Mineweb*. 2013. 'Codelco's US$27 billion Plan Gets Costlier', 24 June. Available at: http://www.mineweb.co.za/mineweb/content/en/mineweb-mining-finance-investment-old?oid=195282&sn=Detail [Accessed November 2013].

129 S. Andersen. 2013. 'The Mineral Industry of Chile', United States Geological Survey. Available at: http://minerals.usgs.gov/minerals/pubs/country/2011/myb3-2011-ci.pdf [Accessed November 2013].

130 *The Wall Street Journal*. 2009. 'Prudent Chile Thrives Amid Downturn', 27 May.

MEXICO

Mexico has the second largest economy in Latin America after Brazil, and has the region's third-highest GDP per capita after Chile and Argentina.[131] It is one of the world's 10 largest oil producers. State-owned Petroleos Mexicanoes (Pemex) has been the sole producer for 75 years.[132] Although Mexico went through its own cycles of privatisation and nationalisation, Pemex has maintained this monopoly as the country has continued with its ban on foreign investment in the industry. Therefore, the country's extractive model results in the state appropriating 100 per cent of the rents from its oil industry for the people of Mexico. Today, Pemex is the world's 12th largest oil company.[133] It has been simultaneously referred to as a 'cash cow' and a 'sacred cow'. As a cash cow, it generated 16 per cent of the country's export earnings in 2011. Earnings from the industry accounted for 34 per cent of total government revenues. As a sacred cow, Pemex has immense and symbolic national importance, which is deeply rooted in Mexico's sense of sovereignty and independence. Increasingly, these two roles are in tension as Pemex struggles to remain a cash cow while subject to the legal and political constraints of a sacred national treasure.[134]

In 1934, Lazaro Cárdenas del Rio was elected president with a mandate to implement progressive social and economic reforms. Although he stabilised the country and implemented numerous social reforms such as the redistribution of land and the expansion of rural education, he is known outside the country for the nationalisation of the oil industry. Following a wave of labour unrest in the oil industry, Cardenas nationalised foreign companies in 1938 and formed Pemex, the national oil company.[135] According to *The New York Times*: 'The popular reaction was spontaneous. To pay the debts incurred by the expropriation of the foreign companies, rich women contributed their earrings, and poor people their chickens.'[136] During its first phase (from 1938 to 1974), Pemex was not viewed as a mass source of revenues for the government. It was not focused on the export market. Its primary mission was to satisfy domestic demand. For the first three decades the company increased production to meet domestic demand. But, after accelerated industrialisation during the late 1960s and early 1970s, Mexico became a net oil importer as production could not meet increased demand.

131 International Monetary Fund. 2013. 'Regional Economic Outlook: Western Hemisphere'. Available at: http://www.imf.org/external/pubs/ft/reo/2013/whd/eng/wreo0513.htm [Accessed November 2013].

132 United States Energy Information Administration. 2012. 'Mexico'. Available at: http://www.eia.gov/countries/analysisbriefsMexico/Mexico.pdf [Accessed November 2013].

133 *Energy Intelligence*. 2013. 'Top 100 Global NOC and IOC Rankings'. Available at: http://www2.energyintel.com/Top100About [Accessed November 2013].

134 T. Samples and J. Vittor. 2013. 'Energy Reform and the Future of Mexico's Oil Industry: The Pemex Bidding Rounds and Integrated Service Contracts', *Texas Journal of Oil, Gas and Energy Law*, Vol. 7.

135 Maurer. 2010. 'The Empire Struck Back: The Mexican Oil Expropriation of 1938 Reconsidered', Harvard Business School. Available at: http://www.hbs.edu/faculty/Publication%20Files/10-108.pdf [Accessed November 2013].

136 *The New York Times*. 2013. 'Mexico's Theology Of Oil', 31 October. Available at: http://www.nytimes.com/2013/11/01/opinion/krauze-mexicos-theology-of-oil.html?pagewanted=all [Accessed November 2013].

During the 1960s, several new oilfields were discovered and Pemex began to make investments in infrastructure to develop them and boost the country's sagging production. After world oil prices soared during the early 1970s, the Mexican government decided to re-start Pemex's export business in 1974. The expansion was financed by external debt and 17 per cent of federal budget expenditures were dedicated to exploration.[137] As a result, production soared during the 1970s and reached 2.1 million bpd in 1980.[138] In 1976, the company struck gold when a fisherman accidentally stumbled upon oil, which turned out to be the huge Cantarell oil field, which started production in 1979. During the early 1980s, a global recession resulted in a collapse in oil prices, sparking a foreign debt crisis in Mexico. The country had no choice but to use its oil industry to refinance and service its debt.

The 1990s saw a partial turnaround in the economy, but Pemex's fortunes did not improve because it had come to play a central role in the Mexican state budget. There was little left for investment after the hefty government take and the company operated with aging infrastructure. It was only after the currency (or peso) crisis in 1994 and 1995 – and the looming threat of a decline in production and therefore government revenue – that the government allowed new large-scale investments in production and, eventually in 2003, exploration.[139] Between 1980 and 2004, production almost doubled to a high of 3.8 million[140] bpd as the government reaped the benefits of 'easy oil' (without investment) from the country's shallow waters in the Gulf of Mexico. Between 1980 and 2008, Mexico extracted 13 billion barrels of oil from Cantarell, which on average accounted for 43 per cent of total production.[141]

During this period, the government became addicted to the benefits of 'easy oil' and could not stop itself from raiding Pemex's finances. The share of oil income as a share of total government revenues reached a high of 42 per cent in 2005.[142] This reached absurd levels in 2012 when Pemex paid taxes of US$69.4 billion (about a third of state revenue) on pre-tax profits of US$69.6 billion, a tax rate of almost 100 per cent. This arrangement has allowed the country to

137 O. Stojanovski. 2008. 'The Void of Governance: An Assessment of Pemex's Performance and Strategy', PESD Working Paper #73. Available at: http://iis-db.stanford.edu/pubs/22156/WP_73,_Stojanovski,_Pemex,_12_Apr_08.pdf [Accessed November 2013].

138 BP Statistical Review Data Workbook. Available at: http://www.bp.com/en/global/corporate/about-bp/statistical-review-of-world-energy-2013.html [Accessed November 2013].

139 O. Stojanovski. 2008. 'The Void of Governance: An Assessment of Pemex's Performance and Strategy', PESD Working Paper #73. Available at: http://iis-db.stanford.edu/pubs/22156/WP_73,_Stojanovski,_Pemex,_12_Apr_08.pdf [Accessed November 2013].

140 BP Statistical Review Data Workbook. Available at: http://www.bp.com/en/global/corporate/about-bp/statistical-review-of-world-energy-2013.html [Accessed November 2013].

141 Bázan and González. 2011. 'Mexican Oil Industry: Shifting to Difficult Oil'. Available at: http://www.worldenergy.org/documents/congresspapers/386.pdf [Accessed November 2013].

142 J. Ros. 2011. 'The Macroeconomic Consequences of Falling Oil Revenues in Mexico: A Looming Crisis or a Mixed Blessing?' James Baker III Institute for Public Policy, Rice University and University of Oxford. Available at: http://bakerinstitute.org/files/533/ [Accessed November 2013].

maintain a relatively low tax take from the rest of the economy.[143] Meanwhile, between 2004 and 2012, production dropped 24 per cent to 2.9 million bpd[144] on the back of plunging output from the aging Cantarell oil field. The country needs to urgently increase investment in the industry. Pemex has to spend US$60 billion a year to unlock new oil and shale gas reserves, according to its CEO Emilio Lozoya, but in 2012 capital expenditure was US$24 billion.[145] In December 2013, Mexico's congress agreed to a constitutional amendment to allow foreign investment in the industry. However, private investment is unlikely to fill the gap entirely. A lower tax rate, to allow Pemex to close its capital expenditure gap, will create a hole in the national budget, which can be filled with a combination of loans and tax increases.

VENEZUELA

According to the BP Statistical Review of World Energy, Venezuela had proven oil reserves of 297.6 billion barrels in 2012, the largest in the world, and equivalent to 17.8 per cent of the world's total.

By comparison, Saudi Arabia, in second position, had proven reserves of 265.9 billion, equivalent to 15.9 per cent of the world's total. There have been significant upward revisions of Venezuelan reserves from 99.4 billion barrels (in 2007) to 172.3 billion barrels (2008) to 211.2 billion barrels (2009) to 296.5 billion barrels (2010) and 297.6 billion barrels (2011). Since 2007, the BP review has upwardly revised Venezuelan reserves by 197.3 billion barrels or almost 200 per cent.[146] The United States Energy Information Administration (EIA) says the upward revisions have been due to the inclusion of massive reserves of extra-heavy oil in Venezuela's Orinoco belt. Reserves could be even bigger at 316 billion barrels, with further investigation from the 'Magna Reserva' project, the agency says. According to the United States Geological Survey (USGS), the mean estimate of recoverable oil resources from the Orinoco Belt is 513 billion barrels of oil.[147]

In 2012, Venezuela was the world's 10th largest producer of oil with an output of 2.7 million bpd, equivalent to 3.5 per cent of the world total. Since 2006,

143 J. Ros. 2011. 'The Macroeconomic Consequences of Falling Oil Revenues in Mexico: A Looming Crisis or a Mixed Blessing?' James Baker III Institute for Public Policy, Rice University and University of Oxford. Available at: http://bakerinstitute.org/files/533/ [Accessed November 2013].

144 *BP Statistical Review Data Workbook*. Available at: http://www.bp.com/en/global/corporate/about-bp/statistical-review-of-world-energy-2013.html [Accessed November 2013].

145 Reuters. 2013. 'Mexico to Keep Pumping Pemex For Tax Money Despite Promised Reforms', 30 October. Available: at http://www.reuters.com/article/2013/10/30/mexico-reforms-pemex-idUSL1N0IBOOI20131030 [Accessed November 2013].

146 *BP Statistical Review Data Workbook*. Available at: http://www.bp.com/en/global/corporate/about-bp/statistical-review-of-world-energy-2013.html [Accessed November 2013].

147 US Energy Information Administration. 2012. 'Country Brief Venezuela'. Available at: http://www.eia.gov/countries/analysisbriefs/Venezuela/venezuela.pdf [Accessed November 2013].

when production reached 3.3m bpd, the output of Venezuela's oil fields has dropped by 611,000 bpd or 18.3 per cent.[148] According to the EIA, the reasons include natural decline at older fields, maintenance issues, and the need for increasing foreign investment.[149] In 2011, the oil sector accounted for almost 12 per cent of GDP, about 95 per cent of export earnings and about 40 per cent of government revenues.[150] The country's extractive regime involves 100 per cent state ownership of Petroleós de Venezuela (PDVSA), which produced about 70 per cent of national output in 2011.[151] The state-owned PDVSA, with revenues of US$124.4 billion in 2012,[152] is the world's fifth largest oil company, according to a recent ranking of the world's top companies.[153] Contrary to popular perceptions, it was not former president Hugo Chavez who nationalised the oil industry, but former president Carlos Andrés Pérez, in 1976. Like President Morales of Bolivia in 2005, Chavez merely changed the terms of the contracts of 16 of the 18 international oil companies (IOCs) that were involved in producing the remaining 30 per cent of the country's output. In 2009, the country took control of 80 crude oil services companies.[154]

In addition, Corporación Venezolana de Guayana Minerven C. A. (CVG Minerven), the government-owned mineral and industrial producer, which is an affiliate of PDVSA, manages the state's 32 operating service agreements (OSAs) with IOCs and eight risk-and-profit-sharing agreements that accounted for 20 per cent of the country's oil production in 2011. Finally, Corporación Venezolana de Petroleós (CVP), a wholly-owned subsidiary of PDVSA, also managed four OSAs that produced and processed extra-heavy crude oil and accounted for about 10 per cent of production. In 2006, former president Hugo Chavez mandated a renegotiation of a minimum 60 per cent PDVSA share in all joint ventures, including OSAs. Eventually, 16 of the IOCs (including Chevron and Shell) complied with the new agreements, while Total and ENI were forcibly taken over.[155] On a see-through basis (after stripping out private shareholders), the state share of the 30 per cent of production by joint ventures is 18 per cent.

148　*BP Statistical Review Data Workbook*. Available at: http://www.bp.com/en/global/corporate/about-bp/statistical-review-of-world-energy-2013.html [Accessed November 2013].

149　US Energy Information Administration. 2012. 'Country Brief Venezuela'. Available at: http://www.eia.gov/countries/analysisbriefs/Venezuela/venezuela.pdf [Accessed November 2013].

150　A. Gurmendi. 2012. 'The Mineral Industry of Venezuela', United States Geological Service. Available at: http://minerals.usgs.gov/minerals/pubs/country/2011/myb3-2011-ve.pdf [Accessed November 2013].

151　US Energy Information Administration. 2012. 'Country Brief Venezuela'. Available at: http://www.eia.gov/countries/analysisbriefs/Venezuela/venezuela.pdf [Accessed November 2013].

152　Bloomberg. 2013. 'PDVA Revenue 2012 Declines as it Sells More Domestic Oil', 22 March. Available at: http://www.bloomberg.com/news/2013-03-22/pdvsa-2012-revenue-declines-as-it-sells-more-domestic-oil.html [Accessed November 2013].

153　Energy Intelligence. 2013. 'Top 100 Global NOC & IOC Rankings'. Available at: http://www2.energyintel.com/PIW_Top_50_ranking_about [Accessed November 2013].

154　A. Gurmendi. 2011. 'The Mineral Industry of Venezuela', United States Geological Service. Available at: http://minerals.usgs.gov/minerals/pubs/country/2010/myb3-2010-ve.pdf [Accessed November 2011].

155　US Energy Information Administration. 2012. 'Country Brief Venezuela'. Available at: http://www.eia.gov/countries/analysisbriefs/Venezuela/venezuela.pdf [Accessed November 2013].

Therefore, the state's direct share of the whole industry is 88 per cent and the private share is 12 per cent. The indirect share also increased because the government increased maximum taxes to 50 per cent from 36 per cent and royalties were increased to more than 30 per cent from one per cent.[156]

Venezuela first discovered oil in 1918. Since then, as Tucker (2004) points out: 'Venezuelan oil history can be best summarised as an ongoing struggle to establish the state's landlord status, and its taxation and regulatory rights over a natural resource in its eminent domain, a struggle waged against the liberalising tendencies of the elite and US imperial interests. Initially, exploration and extraction was leased out and the state collected very little in taxes and royalties. An attempt by the administration of the then president Juan Vicente Gomez to change the policies, resulted in a hodgepodge of regulatory models that led to a proliferation of small concessions to various international and local companies, many of which had been negotiated with concession dealers, some of whom were friends of the dictator. Under this system, the tax take was modest. By 1943, Venezuela obtained US backing for a hike in the royalty rate paid by Standard Oil, Shell and Gulf Oil, which together owned nearly all the concessions in the country'.[157]

The state ended the concession-dealing trade and started playing a more direct bargaining role in the industry. A new national debate resulted in a new policy of 50-50 profit sharing with concessionaires, who also paid a lower tax rate. The policy was a farce because of the accounting tricks used by the concessionaires. By the 1970s, the political mood had changed, with many people calling for an end to oil concessions.[158] On 1 January 1976, President Carlos Andrés Pérez nationalised the industry and created PDVSA. The hope was that nationalisation would facilitate more revenue collection. However, PDVSA became increasingly independent and resisted government oversight through 'internationalisation' – investing oil rents in overseas ventures to avoid transferring the money to the government. For example, PDVSA bought Citgo, a US network of refineries and 14,000 gas stations. The state-owned oil company PDVSA says US$14 billion went out of the country to finance acquisitions in the years of deep economic crisis in Venezuela.[159] According to Tucker (2004), there was a deliberate policy of fiscally asphyxiating the state. To others, the company had become a 'state within a state' that assumed the role previously held by IOCs. Many people feared that PDVSA officials

---

156 I. Torres. 2007. 'The Mineral Industry of Venezuela', United States Geological Service. Available at: http://minerals.usgs.gov/minerals/pubs/country/2005/myb3-2005-ve.pdf [Accessed November 2013].

157 Tucker. 2004. 'Oil State in Revolt: Chavez, Venezuela and US Reaction', Centre for Economic Policy and Research. Available at: http://www.networkideas.org/feathm/feb2004/Todd_Tucker_Paper.pdf [Accessed November 2013].

158 Ibid.

159 PDVSA website. 'Oil Sovereignty: PDVSA Belongs to the People'. Available at: http://www.pdvsa.com/index.php?tpl=interface.en/design/salaprensa/readesp.tpl.html&newsid_obj_id=9975&newsid_temas=54 [Accessed November 2013].

viewed themselves as part of a global managerial network, whose decisions reflected international concerns rather than Venezuelan interests.[160]

As a result, oil did not contribute significantly to development or poverty reduction during this period. By 1989, at the behest of the International Monetary Fund (IMF) and the US Treasury Department, the Venezuelan government implemented Apertura Petrolea, or oil opening. While PDVSA remained state-owned, the industry was opened up to external investment under generous conditions.[161] The policies facilitated the creation of 32 OSAs and four strategic associations, each operated by a non-PDVSA entity. Tucker (2004) concluded that the Venezuelan state was in an advanced state of decay by the early 1990s. The traditional political parties and labour unions had been discredited and the country was accepting Washington's policy dictates in everything from oil production to macro-economic policy.[162]

The overall impression of the period from the 1920s to the 1970s is one of a somewhat turbulent political environment and a chaotic and indecisive public sector that somehow managed to gradually increase the government take from the oil sector, despite the lack of a national vision and consensus about the role of the industry. The country appeared to achieve steady progress. According to Rodriguez (2009), during the 55-year period starting in 1920, Venezuela was the fastest-growing economy in Latin America with a per capita GDP growth rate of 3.97 per cent a year. By 1977 Venezuela was by far the richest nation in Latin America with a GDP per capita 2.1 times the regional average.[163] However, an economic growth collapse had already started. Between 1978 and 1998, GDP per capita declined by 21.5 per cent.[164] Economists attribute the growth collapse to declining per capita fiscal oil revenues – the inability to extract economic rent from the sector. Per capita fiscal revenues rose steadily until the 1970s when they started declining. By the 1990s, they had reached less than one third of their 1970s value – lower than any period since the 1940s.[165] This period of decline coincides with the phases of 'internationalisation' and Apertura Petrolea.

160   T. Miguel. 2005. 'Fueling Concern: The Role of Oil in Venezuela', *Energy*, Vol. 26 (4). Available at: http://www.questia.com/library/journal/1G1-129463344/fueling-concern-the-role-of-oil-in-venezuela [Accessed November 2013].

161   Albert Views. 2006. 'Venezuela and Canada's Very Different Approach to Oil', 14 December. Available at: http://venezuelanalysis.com/analysis/2138&gt%3b [Accessed November 2013].

162   Tucker. 2004. 'Oil State in Revolt: Chavez, Venezuela and US Reaction', Centre for Economic Policy and Research. Available at: http://www.networkideas.org/feathm/feb2004/Todd_Tucker_Paper.pdf [Accessed November 2013].

163   Rodriguez and Gomolin. 2009. 'Anarchy, State and Dystopia: Venezuelan Institutions Before the Advent of Oil', *Bulletin of Latin American Research* 28 (1). Available at: http://frrodriguez.web.wesleyan.edu/docs/working_papers/Anarchy_State_and_Dystopia.pdf [Accessed November 2013].

164   Weisbrot, Ray and Sandoval. 2009. 'The Chavez Administration at 10 Years: The Economy and Social Indicators', Centre for Economic Policy and Research. Available at: http://www.cepr.net/documents/publications/venezuela-2009-02.pdf [Accessed November 2013].

165   Hausman and Rodriguez. 2006. 'Why Did Venezuelan Growth Collapse?' In Hausman and Rodriguez (eds.) *Venezuela: Anatomy of a Collapse*. Available at: http://www.cid.harvard.edu/events/papers/0604caf/Hausmann_Rodriguez.pdf [Accessed November 2013].

Chavez was elected president in December 1998, and took office in February 1999 with a mandate to reverse the decline. His developmental policies were met with staunch resistance from conservative elites who engaged in economic sabotage.[166] An unsuccessful military coup in April 2002, supported by the elites and a crippling oil sector shutdown and strike from December 2002 to February 2003, resulted in a severe recession that saw GDP decline by 28.1 per cent from the fourth quarter of 2001 to the first quarter of 2003.[167] However, after the strike, the government took control of PDVSA and placed oil revenues at the service of its developmental agenda. The 're-nationalisation' of PDVSA, combined with an increase in government's stake in joint ventures and increases in taxes and royalties collected from IOCs, provided significant funding for social programmes. The government redefined PDVSA's role to include spending at least 10 per cent of its investment budget on social programmes.

The timing was fortuitous because it coincided with a significant increase in world oil prices, which increased from a 22-year low of US$19.30 a barrel (in 1999 just after Chavez became president) to US$99.70 in 2008. As a result, between the first quarter of 2003 and the fourth quarter of 2008, real GDP nearly doubled. PDVSA invested US$56.3 billion into social missions between 2001 and 2009. The percentage of households living in poverty declined by more than half, from 54 per cent in the first half of 2003 to an estimated 26 per cent at the end of 2008.[168] The percentage of households living in extreme poverty declined by 72 per cent to seven per cent.[169] The global financial crisis (GFC), which started in September 2008, resulted in a sharp drop in commodity prices. World oil prices crashed from a high of US$144 a barrel in July 2008 to a low of US$33 in December 2008. The annual average oil price dropped from US$91 in 2008 to US$53 in 2009.

Venezuela went into a recession. The economy declined by 3.2 per cent in 2009 and 1.5 per cent in 2010. Weisbrot, et al. (2009) say the collapse could have been avoided if the country had not implemented mistaken macro-economic policies. Venezuela's fiscal policy was too conservative after the onset of the GFC. It implemented an austerity programme at the wrong time – cutting spending as the economy slid into recession – and for no reason, given its then very low debt to GDP ratio of 20 per cent. Further, the government's biggest

166 *Venezuelanalysis.com.* 2009. 'Venezuela Broke', 12 June.

167 Weisbrot, Sandoval and Rosnik. 2006. 'Poverty Rates in Venezuela, Getting the Numbers Right', Centre for Economic Policy Research (CEPR). Available at: http://www.cepr.net/documents/venezuelan_poverty_rates_2006_05.pdf [Accessed November 2013].

168 Weisbrot, Ray and Sandoval. 2009. 'The Chavez Administration at 10 Years: The Economy and Social Indicators', Centre for Economic Policy and Research. Available at: http://www.cepr.net/documents/publications/venezuela-2009-02.pdf [Accessed November 2013].

169 Ibid.

long-term economic policy mistake had been to allow its exchange rate to become significantly overvalued over the previous seven years. The economy, however, recovered, and grew by 4.2 per cent in 2011 and 5.6 per cent in 2012, as government spending picked up, led by the implementation of a mass housing programme.[170]

Venezuela has oil reserves of up to 500 billion barrels. It is only producing one billion barrels a year. There is no reason why it cannot produce more and become a developed country within a very short time. This case study illustrates the fact that a developmental extractive regime must take place within the context of coherent macro-economic policies. The problem is not the extractive regime, per se, but the propensity of the ruling United Socialist Party of Venezuela (PSUV) under former president Chavez and current president Nicolas Maduro to commit macro-economic policy errors, the latest of which is to allow a currency crisis to emerge.

In 2013, a black market emerged in which the dollar fetched seven times the official rate. This drove inflation up to 50 per cent and resulted in shortages of consumer goods. But how can it be that a country with oil revenues of US$93 billion in 2012, a current account surplus of US$11 billion and foreign exchange reserves of US$36.7 billion can allow such a situation to emerge?[171] The country had the resources to eliminate the black market and reverse the inflation spiral. Finally, Venezuela must find an appropriate balance between using oil revenues to pursue broader developmental objectives and investing in the industry. The country must develop an institutional mechanism to increase investment in the industry and achieve a significant increase in production.

CONCLUSION

In Latin America over the past century, the economic policy pendulum has swung wildly between the extremes of privatisation and nationalisation. Political instability in many countries exacerbated the policy swings. By the early 1990s many countries had been through five privatisation-nationalisation cycles. During the new millennium, a 'pink-tide' of left-leaning leaders reversed the privatisation policies of the 1990s. Although left-leaning leaders are probably more likely to introduce policies to extract a higher share of natural resources rents, it is difficult to argue that such policies are motivated by ideology. It

170 Weisbrot, Ray and Sandoval. 2009. 'The Chavez Administration at 10 Years: The Economy and Social Indicators', Centre for Economic Policy and Research. Available at: http://www.cepr.net/documents/publications/venezuela-2009-02.pdf [Accessed November 2013].

171 *The Guardian*. 2013. 'Long Awaited Apocalypse Not Likely in Venezuela', 7 November. Available at: http://www.cepr.net/index php/op-eds-&-columns/op-eds-&-columns/long-awaited-apocalypse-not-likely-in-venezuela [Accessed November 2013].

seems as if most leaders wanted a fair and equitable share of natural resource rents. In Argentina, President Christina Fernandez bought back 51 per cent of the shares of YPF with the aim of reducing a fuel trade deficit, which was blamed on a lack of investment by the company's former owners. In Bolivia, citizens protested against the excesses of two decades of neo-liberal reforms that had resulted in declining per capita incomes. They voted in a referendum to nationalise the hydrocarbon sector, refund the state-owned YPBF and increase tax and royalty rates on the IOCs. A president was forced to resign when he failed to implement the reforms that the people had voted for. When Evo Morales was elected president six months later in December 2005, he had no choice but to implement the reforms. However, he did not nationalise the IOCs; he merely changed the terms of their contracts to what existed before the neoliberal reforms of his predecessors.

In Brazil, Petrobrás, the national oil company, was established in 1953 after a lengthy period of democratic debate, which included discussions with political parties and the public, which was won by a nationalist faction's 'The Oil is Ours' campaign.[172] At the time, the country was producing less than 3,000 bpd. It took 60 years to reach 2 million bpd.

In Chile, although a socialist president (Salvador Allende) nationalised the country's copper industry, it was a ruthless dictator, a believer in free-market economics (Augusto Pinochet), who created CODELCO, the national copper company, while he privatised more than 400 companies that had been nationalised by his predecessor.

In Mexico, President Lazaro Cardenas nationalised the oil industry in 1938 because of the intransigence of the oil companies who refused to improve the shocking conditions suffered by workers. In a speech announcing the nationalisation he said: 'In how many of the villages bordering the oil fields is there a hospital, or school, or social centre, or a sanitary water supply, or an athletic field, or even an electric plant fed by the millions of cubic metres of natural gas allowed to go to waste?'[173]

In Venezuela, contrary to popular perceptions, former president Hugo Chavez did not nationalise the oil industry. Former president Carlos Andrés Pérez nationalised the industry in 1976 to capitalise on a quadrupling of world oil prices after the middle-east oil embargo. A 'socialist', he paid US$1 billion to buy the foreign companies, signed the papers with a golden pen and then implemented

---

172 R. Da Motta, A. Aragao and J. Mariano. 2008. 'Hydrocarbons in Latin America – Case of Brazil'. Available at: https://www.google. co.za/search?q=hyrdocarbons+in+latin+america+case+of+brazil&ie=utf-8&oe=utf-8&rls=org.mozilla:en-US:official&client=firefox-a&gws_rd=cr&ei=3jTlUrTyCo2BhAfvrlHgDw# [Accessed January 2014].

173 http://global.oup.com/us/companion.websites/9780195375701/pdf/SPD7_Nationalization_Mex_Oil.pdf [Accessed January 2014].

a US$53 billion public works programme, which included a subway in Caracas and a music programme for the poor.[174] As the country boomed, business deals were reportedly discussed at the mansion of his mistress, who wore a gold replica of an oil tower on a chain around her neck. Perez returned to the presidency as a 'Thatcherite' in 1989, implementing a brutal IMF structural adjustment programme. It was an eventful period which included riots against the IMF programme in which 400 people died, two coup attempts, one of which was led by lieutenant-colonel Hugo Chavez who was imprisoned, and ended with the impeachment and house arrest of the president in 1993 for diverting US$17 million of public money to a secret fund.[175]

The impact of natural resource policies on the economy is highest in countries where extractive industries are a significant part of the economy. There is less impact on the economy in countries such as Argentina and Brazil where extractive industries are a smaller part of the economy. In Argentina, mineral fuels accounted for about 6 per cent of total exports in 2012, which indicates their limited role in the country's economy. In Bolivia, oil and gas accounted for 5.9 per cent of GDP, 30 per cent of government revenues and 45 per cent of exports.[176] So the decision to renegotiate the contracts of the IOCs in 2006 to capture a higher share of rents reduced dividend outflows, and resulted in higher revenues for the government, which were re-invested in the economy. Income from oil and gas increased from US$173 million in 2002 to more than US$2.2 billion in 2011.[177] The economy grew by 4.8 per cent a year between 2006 and 2012. By comparison, real GDP per capita declined between 1950 and 2000.

Brazil is a major producer of hydrocarbons (oil and gas) and minerals (mostly iron ore). In 2010, the two sectors accounted for 29.8 per cent of the country's total exports. However, Brazil has a relatively low ratio of exports to GDP of about 13 per cent.[178] As a result, the combined contribution of the country's extractive industries to GDP was just above 3 per cent in 2010. The contribution to employment was 300,000 in 2009, less than one per cent of the country's labour force, with mining accounting for 232,000 jobs. This reflects the highly capital-intensive nature of these extractive industries.[179] Although oil and

174 *The Economist*. 2011. 'Carlos Andres Perez', 6 January. Available at: http://www.economist.com/node/17848513 [Accessed January 2014].

175 *The New York Times*. 2010. 'Carlos Andres Perez, Former President of Venezuela, Dies At 88', 26 December. Available at: http://www.nytimes.com/2010/12/27/world/americas/27perez.html [Accessed January 2014].

176 US Energy Information Administration. 2012. 'Country Brief Bolivia'. Available at http://www.eia.gov/countries/cab.cfm?fips=BL [Accessed on 14 November 2013].

177 B. Kohl and L. Farthing. 2012. 'Material Constraints to Popular Imaginaries: The Extractive Economy and Resource Nationalism in Bolivia', *Political Geography* Volume 31, Issue 4, May, pp. 225–235. Available at: http://www.sciencedirect.com/science/article/pii/S0962629812000212 [Accessed November 2013].

178 Information obtained from http://www.quandl.com/economics/exports-as-share-of-gdp-all-countries [Accessed January 2014].

179 International Council on Mining and Metals. 2013. 'The Mining Sector in Brazil: Building Sustainable Institutions for Sustainable Development'. Available at: http://www.google.co.za/url?sa=t&rct=j&q=&esrc=s&source=web&cd=7&cad=rja&ved=0CGQQFjAG&url=http%3A%2F%2Fwww.icmm.com%2Fdocument%2F5423&ei=IhHiUuuUDZOShgfGpoD4AQ&usg=AFQjCNFQ-0bVwELqHN4ln7Fp6vZZ1rZZaA&bvm=bv.59930103,d.bGQ [Accessed January 2014].

gas and mining are still a small part of the economy, their role has increased recently. Between 2000 and 2010, there was a 507 per cent increase in the production value of mining from US$10 billion in 2000 to US$50 billion in 2010.[180] Petrobras has announced a US$237 billion investment programme between 2013 and 2017 to develop pre-salt deposits, and to more than double production to 5.7 million bpd by 2020 from 2 million bpd today.

In Chile, copper plays an important role in the country's economy. In 2012, the country produced 5.433 million tonnes of copper, equivalent to 32 per cent of the world's total production. During the same year, copper mining contributed 10.8 per cent to the country's GDP and generated exports of US$42 billion, equivalent to 53 per cent of total exports. State-owned CODELCO, with about one-third of the country's production, paid taxes of US$42.5 billion to the national treasury between 2006 and 2012. In 2012, the copper industry (public and private) paid taxes of US$8.4 billion, equivalent to 14.2 per cent of government revenues. After 1990, the government opened up the industry to foreign multinationals who invested US$15.5 billion in the industry between 1991 and 2003. During this period there was a sharp increase in production to 4.9 million tonnes from 1.6 million tonnes.

In Mexico, President Lazaro Cardenas del Rio nationalised the oil industry in 1938. State-owned Petroleos Mexicanoes (Pemex) was the sole producer for 75 years. Initially, the objective was to satisfy domestic demand. Pemex was not a cash cow. By the mid-1970s, after accelerated industrialisation, the country became an oil importer. The government sanctioned new investments and stumbled upon the giant Cantarrell oil field. Production soared and the government soon became addicted to Pemex's cash flows. By the 1990s, the company had come to play a central role in the Mexican budget. The share of oil income as a share of government revenues reached a high of 42 per cent in 2005. The addiction reached absurd levels in 2012 when Pemex paid taxes of US$69.4 billion (a third of state revenue) on pre-tax profit of US$69.6 billion, a tax rate of almost 100 per cent. Starved of investment, production dropped by 24 per cent to 2.9 million bpd between 2004 and 2012. In December 2013, Mexico's congress agreed to a constitutional amendment to allow foreign investment in the industry.

---

180 International Council on Mining and Metals. 2012. 'The Role of Mining in National Economies'. Available at: http://www.icmm.com/the-role-of-mining-in-national-economies [Accessed November 2013]. International Council on Mining and Metals. 2013. 'The Mining Sector in Brazil: Building Sustainable Institutions for Sustainable Development'. Available at: http://www.google.co.za/url?sa=t&rct=j&q=&esrc=s&source=web&cd=7&cad=rja&ved=0CGQQFjAG&url=http%3A%2F%2Fwww.icmm.com%2Fdocument%2F5423&ei=IhHiUuuUDZOShgfGpoD4AQ&usg=AFQjCNFQ-0bVwELqHN4ln7Fp6vZZ1rZZaA&bvm=bv.59930103,d.bGQ [Accessed January 2014].

In Venezuela, Hugo Chavez was elected President in 1998. The national oil company, PDVSA, had pursued an independent internationalisation agenda – investing oil rents overseas to avoid transferring money to the government. After a costly strike and coup attempt, the government took control of the already nationalised company in 2003 and placed oil revenues at the service of a developmental agenda. He also changed the terms of the contracts of 16 of the 18 International oil companies (IOCs), which were involved in producing 30 per cent of the country's output.[181] With a greater share of oil rents, and helped by rising world oil prices, the economy nearly doubled between the first quarter of 2003 and the fourth quarter of 2008, and the poverty rate fell to 26 per cent from 54 per cent over the period. In 2011, Venezuela's oil sector accounted for almost 12 per cent of GDP, 95 per cent of export earnings and 40 per cent of government revenues.[182]

181 A. Gurmendi. 2011. 'The Mineral Industry of Venezuela', United States Geological Service. Available at: http://minerals.usgs.gov/minerals/pubs/country/2010/myb3-2010-ve.pdf [Accessed November 2011].

182 A. Gurmendi. 2012. 'The Mineral Industry of Venezuela', United States Geological Service. Available at: http://minerals.usgs.gov/minerals/pubs/country/2011/myb3-2011-ve.pdf [Accessed November 2013].

CHAPTER 4: MIDDLE EAST, NORTH AND NORTH-EAST AFRICA

INTRODUCTION

The manner in which resource nationalism is defined is often coloured by the ideological framework on which the process is based. Many early nationalisation projects by states in the Middle East and Africa gained popular support as they sought to define the state as independent of foreign ownership. This is crucial when one considers that, by the end of the 1960s, 85 per cent of the world's oil reserves were in the hands of a small group of multinational companies.[183]

Following the Asian financial crisis of 1998, which was caused by the implementation of extensive neoliberal policies reliant on foreign investment for economic growth, resource nationalism regained popularity. The use of central state companies to manage the oil industry has changed the landscape of the oil industry to the extent that the major oil companies are no longer the only key players in the oil game.

It is important to note that the cyclical nature of resource nationalisation as a centre of economic power periodically swings from the international oil companies (IOCs) to the state and its national oil companies (NOCs), and then back to the IOCs in what has been called the 'Obsolescing Bargaining Model' (OBM). The model was developed by Raymond Vernon in 1971 in order to make sense of the movement of ownership between multinational corporations and national governments.[184] Vernon argued that leverage shifts from IOCs to the state, as the former's assets are taken over and the regulatory environment is changed, favours the state. However, as maintenance and expansion projects are often postponed by governments for various reasons, including the need to spend national funds on other sectors, coupled with a lack of skilled personnel, NOCs are then able to renegotiate contracts with weaker state institutions.

Today, oil politics continues to set the agenda for foreign policies towards the Middle East and North Africa region and remains perhaps the single most potent force in defining the longevity of political administrations in that region.

---

183 Heinrich Boll Stiftung Southern Africa. 'Marginal oil: What is driving oil companies dirtier and deeper?' http://www.za.boell.org/web/cop17-698.html [Accessed 12 May 2014].

184 Raymond Vernon. 1971. *Sovereignty at Bay: The Multinational Spread of US Enterprises*, New York: Basic Books.

From Baghdad to Algiers, oil has played an extremely significant role in shaping the political and socio-economic destinies of the region, and the use of politics as a weapon for economic control is seen as imperative in the face of resource nationalism policies undertaken by countries of the Middle East and the global South.

EVOLUTION OF RESOURCE NATIONALISM IN THE MIDDLE EAST

'It's the Oil, stupid,' said Noam Chomsky in 2008 in his analysis of the relationship between the United States and Iraq, in which he astutely summed up the importance of energy resources in the Middle East in redefining the political and economic landscape of the region.[185] As previously noted, statistics broadly suggest that at least half of the world's proven oil reserves are located in the Middle East. This excludes North Africa and countries that have not yet come on-stream, such as those in Somalia's contested region of Puntland, Ethiopia, and vast areas located in both Sudan and South Sudan, that are yet to be explored. A source of incredible wealth, the discovery of 'black gold' has, until the 1970s, been the preserve of Western transnational companies with little accountability or responsibility to the nations from which these resources and minerals were extracted.

The early years of the twentieth century were characterised by competition between colonial powers for control over territory and resources to feed the new and increased appetite for manufactured goods. As the nascent automobile industry took off in the United States and the realisation dawned that petroleum was essential to economic growth and influence, the colonial powers and the USA engaged in wars of expansion and influence which proved to be unsustainable. In an attempt to redirect their energies from competition to mutual benefit, the directors of three major oil companies agreed on a system that would see them divide and rule the already colonised resource-rich regions in the Middle East and North Africa. In August 1928, Royal Dutch Shell, Standard of New York, and Anglo-Persian Oil signed an agreement that in effect created an oil cartel that would be responsible for regulating the price and profit of oil globally. The agreement was based on the creation of the US Gulf Basing Point system that reasoned that, since more than 70 per cent of oil at the time was sourced from the US Gulf, a standard price was set irrespective of whether it was sourced from within or outside of America.[186]

The cartel was able to amass great profits as its constituent companies extracted

---

185 Noam Chomsky. 2008. 'It's the Oil, Stupid!', *Khaleej Times*, 8 July.
186 Albert Clo. 2000. *Oil Economics and Policy*. Massachussets: Kluwer Academic Publishers, p. 76.

petroleum under generous contracts entered into with the colonial regimes controlling the countries of the region, which granted the companies free reign over oil producing territory. Tellingly, the 1928 agreement was only made public some three decades later during an American Senate investigation into the oil industry. In an instructive documentary on the 'Seven Sisters', Al Jazeera reported that as much as 85 per cent of the world's oil reserves were controlled by the seven major companies by the end of the 1960s.

The political de jure independence of countries in Africa and the Middle East from colonial control that began in the 1950s soon embraced the concept of economic sovereignty and nationalisation and quickly became a rallying point within the industrialising world. It was not long before governments and the populations of these countries saw foreign ownership and control over their resources as a major obstacle to economic development. And it was during this period that African and Middle Eastern models of socialism were also experimented with in an attempt to develop economies that were still strongly rooted in dependence on their former colonial rulers. In March 1951, under the first democratically-elected president, Mohammad Mossadegh, Iran became the first country in the region to create a national oil company – to the chagrin of the cartel that had been extracting and profiting from Iranian oil in the early twentieth century.

A move as dramatic as the nationalisation of Iran's oil fields would have proven to be too extreme for Britain. In an interesting mirroring of recent sanctions against Iran, an embargo of Iranian oil was implemented by Britain. It punished buyers of Iranian oil and thereby choked the national company. In addition, Britain withdrew technical personnel crucial to the maintenance and operation of the Iranian refineries. With the help of the American CIA, the British government under Churchill orchestrated a coup d'état that replaced Mossadegh with the dictatorial Reza Shah Pahlavi, who proved to be entirely compliant to British and Western desires and plans over his country. Opponents of the coup were killed and, underlying the importance of maintaining the oil status quo, Mossadegh was sentenced to death but later exiled. The events following the Iranian oil embargo were pivotal to the process of opening up Iranian oil fields to US companies.

During Pahlavi's reign, British interests remained intact and the possibility of Iran falling within the Soviet sphere, a constant fear for the British, was contained. Declassified CIA documents attest to the involvement of the USA and the UK in planning and executing the coup, whose legacy has been a deep sense of mistrust of the West among ordinary Iranians and their political elites.[187] Nationalist sentiment and popular support for increased state involvement in

---

187 Department of State. 1972. 'Intelligence Note: Iranian Oil Negotiations', 6 December. Declassified 21 June 2006.

the oil industry was accelerated by the Arab-Israeli war of 1967. In June of that year, Egypt and Syria launched an attack on Israel with a view to halting its encroaching occupation of Palestine and its role in assisting the British and French during the 1956 Suez crisis when pan-Arabism was at its height. Israel defeated the attack with devastating results for the region. It seized control of the Gaza strip, the West Bank, East Jerusalem, Egypt's Sinai Peninsula and the Syrian Golan Heights.

In response to tacit US and British support for Israel during the 1967 Arab-Israeli war, Arab oil producers used their resources as a means of effecting change in the West's relations with Israel. In October 1973, members of the Organisation of Arab Petroleum Exporting Countries (OAPEC) agreed to reduce oil output by five per cent. The only dissenter in this was Iraq. This, in turn, led to a spike in the price of oil, a move with far-reaching consequences for the USA and Western Europe. The implementation of the decision began as a reduction in output and progressed to an all-out embargo on oil exports to Europe and the USA. It was called the first 'oil shock', referring to the fact that the USA and Europe had never had to consider increased prices and supply shortages before that.

ROLLING BACK THE STATE

The heady two decades after independence were followed by the triumph of the capitalist economic model as the Cold War had thawed and the globalisation of the means of production had become a reality. The use of the state as the principal means of financial accumulation resulted in decreased efficiency and a loss of faith in centralist economic models. State-run enterprises that had benefited from easy access to credit lines, and buoyed by regulatory environments aimed at protecting the state's monopoly over the industry, came to be seen as a liability to the economy.

During the 1990s, under the influence of the International Monetary Fund (IMF) and the World Bank (WB), neoliberal economics dominated in emerging and developing economies. As a result, many countries in Asia, Africa and the Middle East undertook large-scale privatisation of various sectors of their economies, a move which also led to the reopening of the energy sector to IOCs. Neoliberal economists proposed that economic prosperity would spontaneously result from market competition and increased efficiency as compared to economic planning by the state. Large-scale privatisation and deregulation led to severe reductions in governmental intervention in the economy and state involvement in large corporations and utilities. The production of what were previously regarded as public goods – including electricity, telecommunications, health and welfare – became new sites of competition for transnationals which were presented as less corrupt, apolitical and thus more efficient in service delivery – none of which were necessarily true. This brought international oil corporations back onto the international oil scene, but only until the end of the 1990s. The 1998 Asian financial crisis led economists and governments that had once been enthused with the idea of opening up their economies to the market to consider steering economic growth through nationalisation of, or intervention in, key industries.

From the beginning of the twenty-first century, governments of oil-rich countries have been able to take advantage of the high cost of petroleum. The 'Seven Sisters' are no longer the major players in the great oil game: their dominance has been replaced by that of a new cartel of state corporations. Together with improved technology and new lines of credit from rising economic powers, these states have been developing their own domestic oil corporations. In contrast to the early twentieth century, 80 per cent of global gas and energy reserves are today in the hands of national oil companies.

SAUDI ARABIA

Saudi Arabia has one-fifth of the world's proven oil reserves, is the largest producer and exporter of petroleum in the world, and maintains the world's largest oil production capacity. However, since 2009, when Aramco met its 12 million barrels per day target, it has shifted its focus to alternative energies, particularly solar energy, in an attempt to move beyond a reliance on oil production. Moreover, domestic energy consumption, and petroleum consumption in particular, has risen steadily, encouraging the shift towards renewable energies. In 2009, the country was ranked 13th in global consumption trends. It is clear that further increases of domestic energy consumption will have a substantial and significant impact on Saudi Arabia's export levels.

Historically, IOCs have had the upper hand in the downstream operations of the hydrocarbon industry through maximising their global distribution networks. However, this function has also been strengthened in NOCs as they take advantage of new technologies and partnerships with other NOCs. Aramco has foreign refinery capacity of up to 2 million barrels per day through joint and equity ventures in the USA, South Korea, Japan and the Philippines. As far as gas is concerned, Saudi Arabia does not export gas and has generally maximised what is called 'associated gas' – gas released as part of the petroleum extraction process – for its domestic purposes. Two factors are placing a strain on the gas sector in the kingdom. The first is that consumer demand is rapidly increasing. The US Energy Information Administration estimates that demand will double its 2011 levels by the year 2030. The spike in demand is due to the fact that the price of gas is comparatively low because of government subsidies that were set when associated gas was plentiful. The second factor relates to the capping of oil production levels, which will mean a decrease in available associated gas. The Persian Gulf area has been earmarked as the main area of natural gas extraction for the kingdom, and it has embarked upon a five year developmental plan to increase its natural gas reserves.

Legal Framework

Two Saudi ministries are responsible for the regulation and oversight of the oil and gas industry: the Ministry of Petroleum and Mineral Resources, and the Supreme Council for Petroleum and Minerals. The latter is composed of members of the royal family, industry leaders and government ministers, and is responsible for policy on petroleum and natural gas, including contract review, as well as strategic planning for Saudi Aramco. The ministry is responsible for national planning in the area of petroleum and minerals.

According to Saudi Arabia's petroleum regulations, exploration, drilling and production is closed to foreign-owned companies. Foreign-owned entities may neither own stakes in Saudi Aramco, nor have equity shares. This has been the case since Aramco's transformation to Saudi Aramco in 1980. The restrictions are, however, limited to only upstream activities while the downstream sector has always accepted the participation of IOCs, particularly in the petrochemical sector. Exxon Mobil and Shell are the two largest IOCs in Saudi Arabia, and have 50 per cent equity stakes in refineries with Saudi Aramco.[188]

After its 2005 accession to the World Trade Organisation (WTO), Saudi Arabia was expected to liberalise its energy sector. In 2003, the Ministry of Petroleum announced that it would open the Ghawar area to auction for natural gas exploration. In 2004, Russia's Lukoil, China's Sinopec, Italy's ENI and Spain's Repsol each won a 40-year long concession, marking a significant change in Aramco's nationalisation policy.

It will be challenging for Saudi Aramco to maintain its hegemony over the industry in the face of demographic realities that have seen a steady increase in domestic consumption of energy. Moreover, resource nationalism has changed the global energy landscape and given producer countries in other parts of Asia – most notably China and India – and Russia — significant political and economic muscle. This reconfiguration of power relations in the international arena continues to have a deep impact on consumer nations, particularly in Africa, where infrastructural development projects have often accompanied exploration contracts.

---

188 *Saudi Arabia Company Laws and Regulations Handbook*, p. 161.

IRAN

The first agreement for oil exploration in Iran was signed in 1901 when exclusive rights were given to William Knox D'Arcy to explore for oil throughout the territory.[189] The Anglo-Persian Oil Company (APOC), the forerunner to Iran's national oil company of today, was formed after the discovery of oil in 1908.[190] In 1935, APOC changed its name to the Anglo-Iranian Oil Company (AIOC). Its agreements with the Persian Shah spanned several decades, covered vast parts of the country's territory, and it owned all the oil in Iran. Playing a role as a conduit between the USA and Britain on the one hand, and the Soviet Union on the other, the company was fundamental to the successes of the British during World War II.[191]

However, attempts at engaging the British authorities to include greater Iranian participation at both staff and revenue level began as early as the 1920s. The talks were aimed at reducing taxes on the profits of oil, which was also part of the concessionary deal, and increasing the number of Iranian staff in the AIOC. Not only was the company taking the lion's share of profits, but revenue granted to Iran was further reduced by taxes imposed by Britain. Iranian concerns were disregarded and the conditions under which average Iranian oil workers were expected to work stood in stark contrast to the lavish and cushioned lives of their British counterparts and superiors.

While this was, of course, a hallmark of the colonial experience, it played a big role in strengthening a deep sense of injustice felt by Iranians, a sentiment that was further inflamed after the ousting of the nationalist prime minister, Mohammed Mossadegh, in 1953. The process of decolonisation gave rise to a wave of expectation among the colonised: the expectation of complete delinking from their past of political and economic subjugation. Their sense of nationalism was buoyed by the first UN Resolution on Permanent Sovereignty over Natural Resources that was passed in 1962.

Successive Iranian governments have indeed utilised the oil sector as a means of economic and political survival. In his study of the NIOC and its relationship to the state, Paasha Mahdavi argues that the NIOC 'supplies politically visible goods and services, including a costly but very popular subsidy for gasoline that makes retail energy in Iran nearly free ... [d]espite successful efforts to partly diversify the economy, the country remains in some respects heavily dependent on hydrocarbons.'[192]

---

189 Stephen Kinzer. 2003. *All the Shah's Men: An American Coup and the Roots of Middle East Terror*, p. 48. John Wiley and Sons.
190 Kinzer, p. 48-49.
191 See Mary Ann Heiss. 2001. 'Real Men Don't Wear Pajamas: Anglo-American Cultural Perceptions of Mohammed Mossadeq and the Iranian Oil Nationalization Dispute', in Peter L. Hahn and Mary Ann Heiss, *Empire and Revolution: The United States and the Third World Since 1945*, p. 178–194. Ohio State University Press.
192 Hults, David. R., Thurber. Mark C. and Victor, David G. 2012. *Oil and Governance: State-owned Enterprises and the World Energy Supply*, p. 234. New York: Cambridge University Press.

In 1994, a buy-back contract was introduced as a way of attracting international investment back to Iran. The scheme did not attract as much interest as it was hoped, since the risks tended to outweigh the benefits in the absence of a predictable power-sharing agreement. The Iranian oil industry's success has been variable, with the recent past witnessing dips and climbs in profitability due to various internal and external factors.

Iran's Hydrocarbon Sector

Iranian crude oil is generally categorised as 'heavy, sour, crude', and much of the more easily accessible sources of oil have already been tapped. Moreover, the changing geological landscape has made exploration more difficult as new but less accessible areas show promise of producing oil reserves. One of the most important changes to take place after the revolution was the creation of the Ministry of Petroleum, which introduced a new structure to which the NIOC would be accountable.

Presently, Iran holds the world's fourth largest proven oil reserves, and is second only to Russia with regard to natural gas resources. It has, however, been adversely affected by the international sanctions regime which has been blamed for the decrease in oil production since 2012.

Legal Framework

Iran's energy sector is governed by the Supreme Energy Council, which is chaired by the president. The Council was established in 2001 and consists of ministers of the petroleum, economy, trade, agriculture, mines and industry portfolios in addition to other sector representatives.

The current legislative framework regulating Iran's energy sector is based on the Constitution of the Islamic Republic of Iran, the Iranian Petroleum Act, the Iranian Budget and Plan Code, the Economic, Social and Cultural Development Plan, Foreign Investment Promotion and Protection Act (FIPPA), and related legislation. The energy sector is thus regulated by both direct legislation such as FIPPA and indirect laws related to taxation and labour law.[193]

The Foreign Investment Promotion and Protection Act grants equal status to domestic and foreign investors. However, in the case of expropriation or nationalisation of foreign investments, investors are to be compensated based on the real value of the investment at the time of appropriation. The Act also includes laws related to foreign financing of energy projects, such as a buy-back scheme. The scheme was initiated in 1990 as a means of attracting investment – without violating the Iranian Constitution which explicitly forbids foreign

193   United States Energy Information Agency (EIA). Available at: http://www.eia.gov/countries. [Accessed 15 March 2014].

ownership of hydrocarbon resources. The post-revolution Petroleum Act also emphasises the need for state ownership over Iran's natural resources. The buy-back scheme essentially allows foreign contractors to invest in the exploration and extraction of Iranian oil fields through an Iranian proxy company. The foreign company is compensated for expenses it incurs, in addition to a negotiated fee which allows for the purchasing of Iranian hydrocarbon products.

LIBYA

Since 1969, Libya has largely been associated with its former leader, Muammar Gaddafi, whose flamboyant leadership style always garnered media attention, irrespective of his political beliefs. Libya was governed jointly by the United Kingdom and France until the United Nations General Assembly declared it an independent state in 1951.

Libya's strategic position as a gateway to Africa, the Middle East and Europe became more pronounced after the discovery of oil in 1959. The discovery spurred the development of infrastructure for the export of oil to Europe. By 1961, a 167-kilometre pipeline was ready to pump fuel from Libya's interior oil producing region to the Mediterranean. Production of oil increased dramatically and by 1969 it surpassed 3 million barrels per day.[194]

However, following the course of many oil-rich nations, the initial flood of wealth from petroleum exploitation remained in the hands of the ruling elite. The imbalances and inequality that resulted set the stage for the entrance onto the scene of the nationalist Colonel Muammar Gaddafi, who overthrew the Senussi monarchy in a coup in 1969.

Gaddafi's revolutionary period may be divided into three phases, signifying the ideological waxing of his revolutionary agenda.[195] The first phase, in the immediate post-monarchy environment, involved the reorganisation of the Libyan state. This was followed by the second phase, which involved the development of nationalist policies, influenced by Gamal Abdul Nasser's Arab socialist model. Finally, the third phase involved the creation of a Libyan model of socialism with Gaddafi's *Green Book*[196] as the guiding ideology. In theory, the tract established the state of Libya as the 'rule of the masses', made up of a complicated structure of 'popular committees' at regional and local levels,

194 http://en.wikipedia.org/wiki/Oil_reserves_in_Libya. [Accessed 15 March 2014].

195 Wikioil open source reference. Available at: http://www.investment-hr.com/oil_gas_docs/Libya%20oil%20almanac.pdf from Wikioil open source reference [Accessed 15 March 2014].

196 See Muammar Al Qaddafi, *The Green Book*. Tripoli: Libyan People's Committee, various editions. Available at: https://archive.org/details/TheGreenBook_848 [Accessed 15 March 2014].

as opposed to top-down structures of authority. These committees were to offer citizens opportunities for direct access to decision-making. However, as patronage and clientelism deepened, the popular committees became structures which defended the status quo and Gaddafi's authoritarian rule to the exclusion of any opposition.

In contrast to the Iranian model, Libya followed the 'creeping expropriation' model in which the regulatory mechanisms increasingly shifted the balance in favour of the state. An increase in the price of oil led to major windfall profits for the Libyan state and, in 1970, the first nationalisation took place with the dissolution of the Libyan Petroleum Company (Lipetco). This set the stage for the creation of the Libyan National Oil Company. In addition to nationalising Lipetco's assets, the Libyan government also moved to nationalise the distribution networks, an important part of the supply chain.

Libya's Hydrocarbon Sector

In early 2014, three years after the ousting of Gaddafi in the civil war of 2011, the interim prime minister, Ali Zeidan, fled to Germany after he was unable to intercept a South Korean ship which carried off an estimated 20 million dollars' worth of oil sold to a Korean company by rebels in eastern Libya. These rebels wanted to increase their control of the oil ports as a demonstration of power against the central government in Tripoli. The US navy was approached to intercept the ship after orders from Libyan authorities were disregarded. The future of Libya and its gas and petroleum industry hangs upon a fragile and increasingly disparate coalition of forces reliant on international support to legitimate its authority. Moreover, social pressure to deliver on infrastructure and welfare in the post-Gaddafi era is likely to push the incumbent regime of both government and rebels towards exploiting the hydrocarbon sector to attain maximum financial gain. This is made more attractive by the high demand for gas and oil in Europe, which Libya can meet because of its geographical proximity. Italy has historically been the largest consumer of Libyan oil and gas and this situation is unlikely to change in the near future. What makes the Libyan case all the more precarious in terms of unregulated extraction is the fact that the country's resources remain largely untapped, with estimates suggesting that as little as 25 per cent of the country has actually been explored. The fact that Libya has the largest proven reserves on the African continent (estimated at around 48 billion barrels or 38 per cent) means that the yield from such exploration is likely to be massive.

Prior to the civil war that broke out in 2011, the Libyan government had embarked on a project to rehabilitate 24 depleted oil wells using enhanced oil recovery methods. International sanctions against Libya obstructed the importation of various kinds of equipment that would have allowed better maintenance of the oil wells and would have ensured greater oil outputs than what were being experienced.

Legal Framework

Before the civil war, the energy sector was controlled by the National Oil Company, which was responsible for implementing exploration and production sharing agreements (EPSAs) with foreign companies. It is composed of subsidiaries which include the Sirte Oil Company and the Arab Gulf Oil Company (AGOCO). The latter took a prominent role during the civil war after it split from the NOC and sided with the rebel movements. While the regulations under the fifth Exploration-Production Sharing Agreements (EPSA V) regime were seen by industry analysts as punitive towards IOCs, it was the promise of plentiful light sweet crude oil that motivated investors to remain in the country despite the high costs of engaging in Libya. At present, the vastly increased political risk associated with exploration is a major factor that will weigh on potential foreign and domestic investors.

In the current context, it is unlikely that the Libyan economy will directly benefit from oil sales without sound institutions that will enable the use of oil money for the growth and development of the country as a whole. There is a great risk that the country may become balkanised according to regional affiliations, which will ultimately be a failure for political and economic reform as a whole.

SUDAN

Since its independence from Britain in 1951, Sudan has experienced only brief respite from conflict and war. The civil war between the northern and southern parts of Sudan was fought with different levels of intensity over a period of fifty years (from 1955 to 2005), which has wrought havoc on the economic and social development of the country. In 2011, southerners voted to secede from Sudan and establish South Sudan as a sovereign state. The history of the conflict has been intricately linked to the quest for the control of oil resources and distribution networks.

As the largest country in Africa with vast arable land, access to the Nile waters and its geostrategic position between Africa and the Middle East, Sudan always featured prominently as part of the imperial and colonial projects from the Ottoman rulers to the British.

The tension between the North and South part of the country (and, indeed, between Khartoum and most of the country beyond) was a result of gross underdevelopment and it was significantly exacerbated by the discovery of oil in the 1970s. The first oil exploration attempts started as far back as 1959 when Italy's state-owned oil company, Agip, began drilling in the north-eastern Red Sea area of Sudan. The Italians were followed by other European and American oil majors including Total and Chevron. But exploration over a period of fifteen years was unsuccessful and some companies withdrew from the area. Chevron, however, remained in the country and was the first to discover oil in the area of Muglad in 1979. This was followed by a major oil discovery in an area north of Bentiu in western Upper Nile State in 1980. It was clear that the promise of oil reserves were more likely to be found in southern Sudan which then president, Jaffer Nimeiri, seized upon.

As the Sudanese agricultural economy began to deteriorate due to the high costs of the first civil war (from 1955 to 1972), Nimeiri recognised the prospect of a generous windfall for the Sudanese economy through oil exploration. Nimeiri's overconfidence and the regime's intensifying economic difficulties led him to seek direct control over the newly discovered oil resources in the south. In 1980, he announced plans to redraw the borders between the southern and northern provinces. When this proposal was blocked by the regional government, he conveniently created a new province (al-Wihda, or Unity State) and removed the oil fields altogether from southern administrative jurisdiction.[197]

The redrawing of the Sudanese map was an abrogation of the 1972 Addis Ababa agreement that had ended the first civil war. The agreement had maintained Sudanese unity but gave southern Sudan a degree of political and economic autonomy. The violation of the peace agreement was the catalyst for the return to large-scale civil war between the Sudan People's Liberation Movement (SPLM) of the South, and successive Sudanese regimes. The war only ended in 2005.

During this protracted period of war, the Sudanese government continued with its plans to build a refinery in Port Sudan in the north, a long way from the oil fields of the south. It was oil and the control over its distribution that intensified the southerners' determination for independence.

Indeed, the conflict was further exacerbated by the interests of countries whose oil companies had made considerable investments in attaining concessions in the now conflict-ridden areas. Oilfields became a strategic target for the armed wing of the SPLM. In 1983, three workers from the Chevron company were killed, leading to the withdrawal of the company from Sudan. Its concessions were, however, not ceded, and remained in place to be taken up after the end of the war.

---

197 Ali, Taisier M. and Matthews, Robert O. 1999. 'Civil War and Failed Efforts for Peace in Sudan' in Ali, Taisier M. (ed.) and
Matthews, Robert O., *Civil Wars in Africa: Roots and Revolution*. Quebec: McGill-Queens University Press.

In a changing Cold War environment, the Sudanese regime benefited from the withdrawal of Soviet support to the rebel groups in the south and the regime was able to develop the military strength to turn the tide of war in its favour. As a result, oil companies were again courted for investment; some returned, benefiting the state's war effort. It was clear, however, that popular support for Nimeiri was heavily tested, and he was ultimately overthrown by Sadiq Al Mahdi. While Nimeiri had relied heavily on US support for his incumbency, this was not necessarily so for his replacement. In a move that would recognise the extreme nature of realpolitik in the region, the USA changed its position and gave its full support to the SPLM, which could inherit a new oil-rich state should the war prove it victorious. During this period, Chevron and many other oil companies suspended their operations, resulting in significant losses from capital investments made in oil exploration infrastructure.

The US attempted to isolate Mahdi's regime and reduced its financial and military aid to the Sudanese state. This culminated in a US diplomatic withdrawal from Sudan by 1989. Mahdi was later overthrown by Omar al-Bashir, whose National Islamic Front (NIF) party considered Sudan open for business, particularly to countries which opposed US hegemony. Sudan sought closer ties with Libya, Iran and China, all of which were eager to develop alliances because of their own status as political pariahs as far as the West was concerned. These developments were complicated by the imposition of UN sanctions on Sudan in 1996 and US trade sanctions in 1997. The following year, US president Bill Clinton authorised the bombing of a pharmaceutical company in Khartoum. It was a mix of the regime's reliance on oil wealth for legitimacy and the SPLM's reliance on the USA for support that made peace elusive in the Sudan. Oil companies were not willing to take such risks in the absence of security guarantees for their investments. Canadian and US companies – including Chevron, Arakis and Talisman – bowed to pressure from human rights' groups and, in the case of the former, to its government's assurance of a tax write-off, that led to the withdrawal of those companies from the Sudan. Underdevelopment and a lack of access to markets due to sanctions took a significant toll on the Sudanese oil industry and, consequently, on the economy as a whole.

Recognising that ideology alone would not be enough to maintain its grip as a ruling party, the NIF reorientated its policies towards attracting non-Western investment in the oil sector. The US companies were replaced by Malaysian and Chinese prospectors with the funds, technology and equal thirst for petroleum. It may be argued that the onward move towards developing the oil sector by the Sudanese state was a game changer in attempts towards attaining peace. The Intergovernmental Authority on Development (IGAD), composed of seven East African nations, initiated negotiations between the SPLM and the NIF, which began in earnest in 1994. The negotiations resulted in the signing of the Comprehensive Peace Agreement between the two sides in 2005 and allowed for the secession of southern Sudan through a referendum.

The outcome of the referendum was a foregone conclusion, as problems regarding the sharing of revenue and wealth over the interim period became a sticking point. Moreover, with the death of SPLM leader, John Garang, in an aviation accident in 2006, mutual suspicions dramatically reduced the desire for reconciliation between north and south. In the referendum, which took place in 2011, the south voted for secession. Between 2005 and 2011, major investments from China bolstered the Sudanese oil industry, but it remains reliant on the technological capabilities of investing countries and companies. The 'Seven Sisters' do not have as much of a presence in Sudan as they may have had before the rise of Asian NOCs like China's CNPC and Malaysia's Petronas.

Sudan's Hydrocarbon Sector

Oil remains the mainstay of the economies of Sudan and the new state of South Sudan. According to IMF statistics, as much as 57 per cent of the Sudanese government's revenue and 98 per cent of that of South Sudan is derived from oil exports.[198] The reality is that oil is largely to be found and explored in South Sudan and the disputed areas bordering the two countries. Moreover, the major refinery and export route for Sudanese oil of either origin is located in Sudan's northern port city. This means that political tension between the two states significantly impacts on exportation and extraction processes. One major incident that illustrates the symbiotic nature of oil activities between the two regions took place in 2012 when South Sudan voluntarily shut down oil production due to a dispute over transit fees. The post-secession economy of Sudan has reeled from a significant cut in revenue, and it sought to make up for this loss through high transit fees for fuel on its way to the Port Sudan refinery.

Legal Framework

The Sudanese Ministry of Finance and National Economy (MOFNE) is responsible for regulating oil imports and refinement. The MOFNE sets the regulations by which the petroleum ministry and the Sudan Petroleum Corporation (SPC) abide. The latter is engaged in exploration, production and distribution of petroleum. It purchases oil from the MOFNE and the China National Petroleum Corporation at a significantly subsidised rate. The SPC then subcontracts refineries to refine the oil, which it later sells off to distribution and marketing companies, again at a reduced rate. According to the IMF, Sudan spent 15 per cent of its revenue on government subsidies in 2012, which has meant that the regime's longevity remains tied to the performance

---

198   United States Energy Information Agency (EIA), http://www.eia.gov/countries/ [Accessed 16 March 2014].

of the economy as the majority of Sudanese depend on subsidies in order to survive.

The Sudanese state-owned oil company, Sudapet, was established in 1997 and forms part of the Ministry of Energy and Mining. It has, since its inception, been involved in the negotiation of contracts with IOCs and manages government concessions.

In 2011, Sudapet's southern operations were nationalised by South Sudan, resulting in a takeover of the company's assets by the South Sudanese government. It was a contentious move that added to the already strained relations between the two states. South Sudan accused its northern neighbour of preventing the sale of oil from its northern port and for charging high transit fees for the use of the pipeline and port. By itself, Sudapet does not have the capacity to undertake exploration activities. However, it has a 50 per cent stake in the White Nile Petroleum Operating Company (WNPOC), which operates in Block 5B of the Sudan. Malaysia's Petronas Carigali Overseas owns the other 50 per cent of the WNPOC. The company undertakes joint ventures with Swedish oil company Lundin as well as India's state oil company.

Sudapet also has a shareholding stake with other major Asian NOCs in the Petrodar Operating Company, which took over Chevron's concessions in the south-east of Sudan. Currently, Sudan's oil market is primarily dominated by Chinese interests with an increasing number of bilateral trade agreements being signed by the two states as an indication of the stability of their relationship. With oil bringing in more than 98 per cent of revenue for the state, the continued instability in South Sudan, and the consequent effect it continues to have on the oil industry, is bad news for both the Sudans.

Nationalisation of Sudan's oil industry may be tempting for the regime, considering the high price of oil. However, Sudan lacks the capabilities to take on technical operational responsibility by itself and would benefit from the development of its capacity before any nationalisation can take place. It is also particularly important to remember that the oil-producing areas have now become flashpoints for conflict within South Sudan itself as that country's nascent authority struggles to establish itself as a functional government due to internal factional rivalries. Sudan's fortunes as an oil producer remain tied to the vagaries of South Sudan's politics, and it has sought to attract more IOCs with the technical expertise to explore and develop oilfields within its own border. In this way, the Sudanese regulatory framework focuses less on nationalisation of its petroleum industry and more on joint ventures in which windfall profits could be shared.

Moreover, as a client state of the Gulf countries, Sudan will also be pressured to limit production so as not to decrease the rate for oil on the international market. Much will hinge on the ability of South Sudan to stabilise both its internal politics and its relationship with Sudan.

CONCLUSION

The twenty-first century has seen incredible shifts in the global economy, largely due to the increasing pace of capital-driven growth that requires an ever-increasing amount of energy to sustain itself. The first oil majors, or 'Seven Sisters', used their collective advantage to become a multinational force accountable mainly to shareholders interested in maximising profits. However, as the anticolonial movement gained momentum in the developing world, economic empowerment and sovereignty also became important parts of the nationalist sentiment. It was during the first decades following independence that resource nationalism became a major policy aimed at strengthening the bargaining power of the Third World, and the Middle East in particular. However, various factors, including the use of alternative sources of energy by the main consumers of Middle Eastern oil, led to increased competition and the need for innovation in the petrochemical industry. International oil companies had a technical and distributive advantage over NOCs, and in the 1990s there was a resurgence of private oil companies.

With the dramatic rise of alternative economic centres of power in Asia and Russia, the state has resurfaced as a key player with the creation of new and exceedingly powerful state enterprises. The case of Saudi Arabia, Iran, Libya and Sudan offer unique examples of the various forms in which states have interacted with private capital in the oil business – with very different results. These examples are by no means representative of all the possible configurations that may result from state and capital interaction. However, it is clear that IOCs are having to reinvent themselves to remain competitive within a changed landscape. They may revisit the cartel formula, but this time as an alternative energy conglomerate specialising in renewable sources rather than the limited emphasis on petroleum and gas. It is also possible to envisage a greater role for IOCs in the area of specialised niche operations that are concentrated on the downstream part of the chain, a feature which has already become prominent in some aspects of distribution. Joint ventures between state and private companies may enhance the productivity and profitability for both sides, particularly in minimising risks.

As significant political transformation takes place in the Middle East, North and North-East Africa regions after the 2011 uprisings, newly democratising and transforming states – as well as states such as Egypt, which have either withstood uprisings or have seen successful counter revolutions – will find themselves facing increasing demands for socio-economic betterment from their populations. Democratic governments will have to respond positively in order to deliver on promises they had made and in order to be re-elected. Non-democratic governments will constantly look over their shoulders, remembering that they are not immune to being overthrown by popular uprisings, and thus attempting to provide for their populations more than they had previously done. In such contexts, resource nationalism, in whatever configuration, is not only alluring, but it can be a necessary mechanism to realise development. It is clear that most people – and governments – of the Third World realise that they live in a different era than they did half a century ago, and that in the new context, neither their states nor their natural resources can be sold to the highest bidder or the superpower that provides the highest level of regime protection. State intervention in the extraction and distribution of natural resources will help maintain national sovereignty, and help ensure that the benefits of the wealth beneath the ground accrue to larger sections of the populations in countries that host those resources, rather than just to domestic and foreign elites.

A striking analogy for the relations between producer and consumer countries is offered by Stanislaw, who sees the two as 'too often circling each other like war boxers – with consumers worried about how much oil producers really can (and will) pump, and producers suspicious of how the shift to alternatives could impact demand'.[199] Now is the time for NOCs to begin to address technology gaps between them and IOCs in a way that will make resource nationalism a positive development for both producer and consumer. In the case of oil producers of the Middle East, North and North-East Africa, much will depend on creating and maintaining a sustainable level of political stability.

199 Stanislaw, J. A. 2009. *Power Play – Resource Nationalism, the Global Scramble for Energy, and the Need for Mutual Interdependence*, p. 26. Available at: http://www.deloitte.com/assets/Dcom-UnitedStates/Local%20Assets/Documents/us_er_PowerPlayResourceNationalism_theGlobalScramble_forEnergyWEB_240209.pdf [Accessed 16 March 2014].

CHAPTER 5: EUROPE

INTRODUCTION

Europe comprises 45 countries and territories: Austria, Albania, Andorra, Belarus, Belgium, Bosnia and Herzegovina, Bulgaria, Croatia, Cyprus, the Czech Republic, Denmark, Estonia, Finland, France, Germany, Greece, Hungary, Iceland, Ireland, Italy, Latvia, Liechtenstein, Lithuania, Luxembourg, Macedonia, Malta, Moldova, Monaco, Montenegro, The Netherlands, Norway, Poland, Portugal, Romania, Russia, San Marino, Serbia, Slovakia, Slovenia, Spain, Sweden, Switzerland, Ukraine, the United Kingdom and Vatican City. In 2012, these countries had a combined gross domestic product (GDP) of US$20.2 billion, equivalent to 28.2 per cent of the world economy's total output. The top six countries: Germany (17 per cent of European GDP), France (12.9 per cent), the United Kingdom (12.3 per cent), Russia (10 per cent), Italy (10 per cent) and Spain (6.6 per cent) accounted for 69 per cent of Europe's GDP.[200]

The economies within Europe are diverse in terms of size and average income levels. The top six countries all have economies that are worth more than US$1 trillion but 18 countries had a GDP of less than US$50 billion. In 2012, Norway had a GDP per capita of almost US$100,000, but seven countries (Ukraine, Romania, Belarus, Bulgaria, Serbia, Bosnia and Moldova) had a GDP per capita of less than US$10,000 and of these, three countries (Ukraine, Bosnia and Moldova) had a GDP per capita of less than US$5,000.[201] According to the International Monetary Fund (IMF), 26 of these countries are classified as part of a group of 36 advanced economies, which comprises the world's richest countries. Another 11 countries (Albania, Bosnia and Herzegovina, Bulgaria, Croatia, Hungary, Lithuania, Macedonia, Montenegro, Poland, Romania and Serbia) are classified as part of a group of emerging and developing European countries.[202]

The advanced economies within Europe achieved their status due to steady and unspectacular rates of economic growth over the past two centuries. For most of the world's history, until 1820, there was 'extensive growth' in the world economy in which GDP grew in line with the growth of the population.

---

200 The statistics in this section are obtained from the Appendices to this report where sources are provided. Refer to Table 1.
201 Ibid.
202 International Monetary Fund (IMF) World Economic Outlook Database. Available at: https://www.imf.org/external/ns/cs.aspx?id=28 [Accessed April 2014].

Industrialisation marked the advent of a new phase of 'modern economic growth' or rising per capita output.[203] At the start of the nineteenth century, most regions of the world were at similar levels of economic development. In 1820, according to Maddison (2006), Western Europe, the world's richest region, had a GDP per capita that was three times that of Africa, the world's poorest region.[204]

OVERVIEW OF THE MINING SECTOR IN EUROPE

According to the United Nations Conference on Trade and Development (UNCTAD), there are three categories of minerals: energy minerals, including oil, natural gas, coal and uranium; metallic minerals, including ferrous metals (e.g. iron ore), precious metals (gold, platinum and silver) and base metals (bauxite, aluminium, copper and cobalt); non-metallic minerals including construction minerals, industrial minerals and precious stones (diamonds and gems). Many industrial and construction minerals do not have a sufficiently high value per unit of weight to be marketed and sold on global markets.[205] Therefore, this overview focuses on energy and metallic minerals.

Europe has a territory of 25.1 million km² and that is equivalent to 16.9 per cent of the world's land area. Russia, the world's largest country with a territory of 17.1 million km², accounts for 68 per cent of Europe's land area and 11.5 per cent of the world's land area. Excluding Russia, Europe has a territory of 8.1 million km², equivalent to 5.4 per cent of the world's total land area.[206] Thus, most of the energy and metallic minerals within Europe are located within Russia. Excluding Russia, Europe is an insignificant world producer of most categories of energy and metallic minerals.

Since 2000, there has been a large increase in oil and gas production in Russia and a dramatic decrease in production in the North Sea. In 2012, Europe produced 13.4 million barrels per day of oil, equivalent to 16.8 per cent of world production. Russia, the world's second largest producer (after Saudi Arabia), accounted for 76.3 per cent of European production. There are only six oil producers in Europe. Together, Russia, Norway and the United Kingdom account for 97 per cent of European production. Denmark, Italy, and Romania account for the remaining three per cent. Excluding Russia, Europe accounted

---

203 R. Tilly. 2010. 'Industrialisation as an Historical Process', European History Online. Available at: http://ieg-ego.eu/en/threads/backgrounds/industrialization/richard-h-tilly-industrialization-as-an-historical-process [Accessed April 2014].

204 A. Maddison. 2006. *The World Economy*, OECD.

205 Unctad. 2007. *World Investment Report 2007*, p. 84. Available at: http://unctad.org/en/pages/PublicationArchive.aspx?publicationid=724 [Accessed April 2014].

206 The statistics in this section are obtained from the Appendices to this report where sources are provided. Refer to Table 1.

Resurgent Resource Nationalism? A Study Into The Global Phenomenon | Europe

81

for 3.8 per cent of world production.[207] In 2012, Europe produced 869 billion cubic metres of oil, equivalent to 25.8 per cent of world production. Russia accounted for 68.1 per cent of European production.

There are 10 natural gas producers in Europe. Together, Russia, Norway, The Netherlands and the United Kingdom account for 93 per cent of European production. Ukraine, Romania, Germany, Italy, Denmark and Poland account for the remaining seven per cent. Excluding Russia, Europe accounted for 8.2 per cent of world production.[208] In 2012, Europe produced 1,035 million tonnes of coal, equivalent to 13.2 per cent of world production. Russia, which has the world's second highest reserves (18.2 per cent of world reserves), produced 4.4 per cent of world production and 32.3 per cent of European production. Other producers include Germany, Poland, Ukraine, the Czech Republic and Greece who (together with Russia) account for 82.7 per cent of European production. Excluding Russia, Europe accounts for 8.9 per cent of world production.[209] Finally, in the category of energy minerals: in 2012, Europe produced 4,153 tonnes of uranium (tU), equivalent to 7.1 per cent of world production. Russia accounted for 69.1 per cent of European production. Europe has five uranium producers. Russia and the Ukraine account for 92.2 per cent of European production. The Czech Republic, Romania and France account for the remaining 8 per cent.[210]

Over the past two centuries, there has been a shift of the centre of gravity of global mining. In the 1860s, Europe accounted for more than 60 per cent of the global value of mining production. There was a sharp decline over the next few decades. By 1930, Europe accounted for 20 per cent of global production. The United States' share of global production increased from 10 per cent during the 1850s to a high of 40 per cent by 1940. This was followed by a dramatic decline over the next few decades, similar to the earlier decline in Europe. By 2011, Europe (excluding Russia) and the United States were each contributing only 3.5 per cent and 4.2 per cent respectively of world metal mining by value, whereas six resource-rich developing countries (Chile, Brazil, Peru, South Africa, Zambia and the Democratic Republic of Congo) were contributing a little more than 22 per cent. Of the developed countries, Australia and Canada accounted for 13.3 per cent and 2,6 per cent respectively. Recently, Australia has emerged as a resource giant, mainly because of its growing iron ore industry. China is the second resource giant at 12.7 per cent. 'All of the so

---

207   The statistics in this section are obtained from the Appendices to this report where sources are provided. Refer to Tables 7–10.

208   The statistics in this section are obtained from the Appendices to this report where sources are provided. Refer to Tables 7, 11, 12 and 13.

209   The statistics in this section are obtained from the Appendices to this report where sources are provided. Refer to Tables 7, 14, 15 and 16.

210   The statistics in this section are obtained from the Appendices to this report where sources are provided. Refer to Tables 7, 17 and 18.

called BRICS countries are major mining countries, ranking among the top 10 centres,' the ICMM says.[211] The BRICS countries accounted for 43 per cent of global production of metallic minerals.

RUSSIA

Russia is one the world's major producers of oil (neft in Russian), natural gas and metallic minerals. In 2012, Russia had oil reserves of 87.2 billion barrels, the world's eighth largest. As noted, it was the world's second largest producer (after Saudi Arabia) with production of 10.6 million bpd, equivalent to 12.8 per cent of world production. It accounted for 76.3 per cent of European oil production. The country has natural gas reserves of 1,162 trillion cubic feet - the world's second largest after Iran - equivalent to 17.6 per cent of world reserves. Russia is the world's second largest producer of natural gas (after the United States) with production of 592.3 billion cubic feet, equivalent to 17.6 per cent of world production. It also accounts for 68 per cent of European production.[212]

Russia had total exports of US$525.4 billion, equivalent to 26 per cent of the country's GDP, in 2012. Oil and gas exports of US$352 billion accounted for 67 per cent of total exports. Oil and petroleum product exports of US$284 billion accounted for 54 per cent of total exports.[213] Natural gas exports of US$68.8 billion accounted for 13 per cent of total exports.[214] Oil and gas revenues accounted for more than 50 per cent of the federal budget. According to Kononczuk (2012): 'The income generated from oil sales is much more vital for the Russian budget than tax revenues from the gas sector. Russia exports around 75 per cent of the oil it produces, while only one-third of Russian gas is exported.'

The extractive regime for hydrocarbons includes high taxes and increasing levels of state ownership. The government takes more than 70 per cent of oil revenues.[215] The Ministry of Natural Resources and Ecology is responsible for the political and policy functions. Russia has two professional agencies responsible for regulation and administration of the sector. Rosnedra (the Federal Agency for Subsoil Use) is responsible for issuing licences and approving development

---

211 International Council on Mining and Metals. 2012. 'Trends in the Mining and Metals Industry'. Available at http://www.icmm. com/publications [Accessed April 2014].

212 The statistics in this section are obtained from the Appendices to this report where sources are provided. Refer to Tables 1, 7–13.

213 UN Comtrade Database. Available at: http://comtrade.un.org/pb/FileFetch.aspx?docID=4905&type=country%20pages. [Accessed April 2010].

214 United States Energy Information Administration. 2014. Russia Country Brief. Available at http://www.eia.gov/countries/cab. cfm?fips=rs [Accessed April 2014].

215 W. Kononczuk. 2012. 'Russia's Best Ally: The Situation of the Russian Oil Sector and Forecasts for its Future', Centre for Eastern Studies. Available at: http://www.osw.waw.pl/en/eksperci/wojciech-kononczuk [Accessed April 2014].

plans. Rosprirodnazor (The Federal Service for Supervision of Nature Use) is responsible for the oversight of compliance.[216]

Russia has two national champions. Rosneft, with 69.5 per cent state ownership, has a market capitalisation of US$60 billion and controls about 40 per cent of national oil production.[217] Total state control of oil production, after taking into account state ownership in other producers, is at 46 per cent.[218] Gazprom, with 50 per cent state ownership, has a market capitalisation of US$85 billion and controls 74 per cent of national natural gas production.[219] It could be argued that there is a higher level of effective control over the industry. Vagit Alekperov and Vladimir Bogdanov, the oligarchs who lead Lukoil and Surgutneftegas, the country's two largest private companies, are loyal to President Vladimir Putin's agenda.[220] With domestic capital in firm control of the industry, there is little room for international oil companies (IOCs), who are treated mainly as technology suppliers,[221] although BP owns 19.75 per cent of Rosneft, the national oil company (NOC).

In January 2004, Russia created an oil stabilisation fund to capture excess oil revenues. The fund grew from US$3.73 billion in January 2004 to US$157.4 billion in January 2008. The government then decided to split the fund into two. The National Reserve Fund took over the previous fund's role of stabilising fiscal revenues and assumed a new mandate of financing the budget deficit. The aim of the National Wealth Fund was to provide a cushion for the country's national pension fund. The wealth fund was a quarter of the size of the reserve fund. During the Great Recession, the assets of the reserve fund collapsed by 82 per cent from a high of US$142.6 billion in August 2008, to a trough of US$25.4 billion in December 2010, as it assisted the government in financing its budget deficit. The wealth fund's assets remained the same during the period. When oil and gas prices recovered, the reserve fund's assets increased to US$84.7 billion by February 2013.[222]

In 2012, Russia had coal reserves of 157 billion tonnes, the second highest in the world after the United States.[223] However, production has lagged far behind the reserves. Domestic consumption has dropped 50 per cent over the past two

---

216 King and Spalding. 2012. 'Overview: Russian Oil and Gas Sector Regulatory Regime'. Available at: www.kslaw.com/imageserver/.../RussianOilGas.pdf [Accessed May 2014].
217 Rosneft website: www.rosneft.com [Accessed May 2014].
218 The statistics in this section are obtained from the Appendices to this report where sources are provided. Refer to Table 49.
219 Gazprom website: www.gazprom.com [Accessed May 2014].
220 Gorst. 2007. 'Lukoil: Russia's Largest Company', The James Baker III Institute for Public Policy, Rice University. Available at: bakerinstitute.org/files/3902/ [Accessed April 2014].
221 W. Kononczuk. 2012. *Russia's Best Ally: The Situation of the Russian Oil Sector and Forecasts for its Future*, Centre for Eastern Studies. Available at: http://www.osw.waw.pl/en/eksperci/wojciech-kononczuk [Accessed April 2014].
222 CEIC Data Blog. 2013. 'National Funds of Russia Gain Momentum in 2013'. Available at: http://blog.securities.com/2013/03/national-funds-of-russia-gain-momentum-in-2013/ [Accessed April 2014].
223 The statistics in this section are obtained from the Appendices to this report where sources are provided. Refer to Tables 14–16.

decades because producers cannot compete with regulated natural gas prices, which are kept artificially low.[224] In 2012, the country was the world's fifth largest producer. It produced 354.8 million tonnes, equivalent to 4.4 per cent of world production. In 2012, the country had coal exports of US$13 billion, equivalent to 2.4 per cent of total exports. By comparison, China, with reserves of 114.5 billion (73 per cent of Russia's reserves), is the world's largest producer with production of 3.7 billion tonnes (10 times Russian production).[225] The Russian government has developed a US$126 billion programme to develop the industry and increase production to 450 million tonnes by 2030, when natural gas will no longer be regulated. During this period, the industry is expected to add 505 million tonnes of annual production capacity and shut down mines with a capacity of 380 million tonnes. The government has established liquidation funds, financed by the industry, to relocate workers at depleted mines.[226] Finally, in energy minerals, Russia produced 2,872 tonnes of uranium in 2012, equivalent to 4.4 per cent of world production. This accounted for 69 per cent of European production.[227]

Russia is also a major producer of metallic minerals. According to the ICMM, Russia was the world's fifth largest producer of metallic minerals in 2010 (after Australia, China, Brazil and China). In the same year, the production value of the country's metallic minerals was US$28.7 billion, equivalent to 1.9 per cent of GDP and 6.6 per cent of total exports. Russia accounted for 59.3 per cent of European production of metallic minerals. In 2012, the country had aluminium exports of US$6.4 billion (1.2 per cent of total exports) and nickel exports of US$3.7 billion (0.7 per cent of total exports).[228] Russia has two privately owned national champions in metallic minerals – aluminium producer RUSAL and Norilsk Nickel – which are controlled by the oligarchs, Oleg Deripaska and Vladimir Potanin, respectively.

RUSAL controls the country's production of alumina, bauxite and primary aluminium.[229] Russia produces 8.4 per cent of the world's primary aluminium. RUSAL, which owns 27.8 per cent of Norilsk Nickel, is the world's largest producer of primary aluminium with a market share of nine per cent. It has revenues of US$8 billion and a market capitalisation of US$6.9 billion – less than the value of its shares in Norilsk Nickel because of the depressed state of

224 E. Safirova. 2013. 'The Mineral Industry of Russia', United States Geological Service (USGS). Available at: http://minerals.usgs.gov/minerals/pubs/country/europe.html#rb [Accessed April 2014].

225 The statistics in this section are obtained from the Appendices to this report where sources are provided. Refer to Tables 14–16.

226 E. Safirova. 2013. 'The Mineral Industry of Russia', United States Geological Service (USGS). Available at: http://minerals.usgs.gov/minerals/pubs/country/europe.html#rb [Accessed April 2014].

227 The statistics in this section are obtained from the Appendices to this report where sources are provided. Refer to Tables 17 and 18.

228 The statistics in this section are obtained from the Appendices to this report where sources are provided. Refer to Tables 19–22.

229 E. Safirova. 2013. 'The Mineral Industry of Russia', United States Geological Service (USGS). Available at: http://minerals.usgs.gov/minerals/pubs/country/europe.html#rb [Accessed April 2014].

Resurgent Resource Nationalism? A Study Into The Global Phenomenon | Europe

85

world aluminium markets.[230] Norilsk Nickel, with revenues of US$12 billion and a market capitalisation of US$28,5 billion, has the following shares of world production: nickel (17 per cent), palladium (41 per cent), platinum (11 per cent) and copper (2 per cent).[231] In 2011, Russia produced 12.8 per cent of the world's platinum and 40 per cent of the world's palladium. For other minerals, Russia had the following shares of world production: antimony (3.6 per cent), bauxite (2.3 per cent), copper (4.4 per cent), gold (7.5 per cent), iron ore (3.4 per cent), lead (2.2 per cent), manganese (0.2 per cent), mercury (2.8 per cent), silver (5.8 per cent), tin (0.1 per cent) and zinc (2.2 per cent).[232]

After the break-up of the former USSR in 1991, the oil industry was organised into 301 oil enterprises, which included about 30 regional production associations (oil producers), refineries and retail associations. Most operated as fiefdoms with a general director who reported to the ministry of oil in Moscow. They were usually named after the town in which they were based. A decision was taken to restructure the industry into vertically integrated oil companies (VIOCs). The first stage of the restructuring in 1993 saw the formation of four companies: Lukoil, Yukos, Surgutneftegaz - which were partially privatised with the state retaining some ownership - and state-owned Rosneft.[233] Lukoil, the largest of the new companies, produced 1.1 million bpd in 1995 from four refineries. Yukos produced 719,000 bpd in 1995 from three refineries. Surgutneftegas produced 669,000 bpd in 1995 from one refinery. The three companies only accounted for 42 of the 301 oil enterprises.[234] The remaining 259 companies were left under the stewardship of state-owned Rosneft, which controlled approximately half of the country's oil production.

There was a second wave of privatisation (1993 to 1995) during which oligarchs, who were close to then former President Yeltsin, feasted on Rosneft's assets. The company gave up shares in the majority of its prime assets such as Tyumen Oil (with production of 456,000 bpd in 1995), Sibneft (409,000 bpd), Sidanco (400,000 bpd), Slavneft (266,000 bpd), ONACO (144,000 bpd), Tatneft and Bashneft. By 1996, Rosneft controlled about four per cent of Russian oil production.[235] There was a third wave of privatisation during the infamous 'oil-for-shares' scheme. Ahead of a critical election in 1996, where it was feared that the communists would win, the cash-strapped government

230 RUSAL website: http://www.rusal.ru/en/ [Accessed April 2014].

231 Norilsk Nickel website: http://www.nornik.ru/en/main [Accessed April 2014].

232 The statistics in this section are obtained from the Appendices to this report where sources are provided. Refer to Table 22.

233 J. Henderson. 2012. 'Rosneft – On the Road to Global NOC Status?' Oxford Institute for Energy Studies. Available at: www.oxfordenergy.org/wpcms/wp-content/.../2012/01/WPM_44.pdf [Accessed April 2014].

234 J. Henderson. 2012. 'Rosneft – On the Road to Global NOC Status?' Oxford Institute for Energy Studies. Available at: www.oxfordenergy.org/wpcms/wp-content/.../2012/01/WPM_44.pdf [Accessed April 2014].

235 J. Henderson. 2012. 'Rosneft – On the Road to Global NOC Status?' Oxford Institute for Energy Studies. Available at: www.oxfordenergy.org/wpcms/wp-content/.../2012/01/WPM_44.pdf [Accessed April 2014].
       Global Security website: http://www.globalsecurity.org/military/world/russia/energy-oil-industry.htm [Accessed April 2014].

agreed to pledge its shares in 12 large state-owned companies as security in return for loans worth US$800 million from a consortium of Russian banks, which were already owned by oligarchs. There were auctions to determine which banks would provide the loans. If the government did not repay the loans after President Yeltsin's re-election, the banks would be allowed to auction the shares.

In the resources sector, the government pledged 45 per cent of Yukos (for a loan of US$159 million), 51 per cent of Sibfneft (US$100 million), 51 per cent of Sidanko (US$130 million), 38 per cent of Norilsk Nickel (US$170 million), 5 per cent of Lukoil (US$35 million) and 40 per cent of Surgutneftegaz (US$88.3 million). Yeltsin won the election. But, as expected, the government did not pay. The banks rigged the auctions and gave the shares to their associates.[236] A new set of oligarchs emerged. They included Mikhail Khodorkovsky (Yukos), Roman Abramovich (Si billioneft) and Vladimir Bogdanov (Surgutneftegaz). By 1999, the oil industry was mostly privately owned, but production had plunged to less than 6 million bpd, partly due to a collapse of domestic demand as the economy contracted throughout the 1990s and a lack of investment in the industry since the late 1980s. But the government had retained a 40 per cent shareholding in Gazprom following its earlier privatisation.

The government's policy towards the oil and gas sector changed after the election of President Vladimir Putin in 2000. The objectives were to extract a higher share of hydrocarbon rents through higher taxes and increased levels of state ownership. There are now two major taxes: the tax on the extraction of mineral resources (NDPI), which was introduced in 2002, and the export duty. The NDPI is a flat tax, which reaches US$15 per barrel. The export duty is a tax on the value of oil above US$25 a barrel. At a price of US$50, the government take (from both taxes) is 55.9 per cent. At a price of US$100, the government take is 71.4 per cent. The criticism of the taxes is that they make it unprofitable to develop 90 per cent of new fields and 30 per cent of the fields already in operation.[237]

In terms of state ownership, the government first considered a merger between Rosneft and Gazprom. However, the plan changed after Yukos was bankrupted and its assets sold to recover a tax liability. Rosneft paid US$9.35 billion to buy Yuganskneftegas, Yukos' prime asset. It later picked up other Yukos assets – Samareneftegas and Tomskneft. Rosneft became the country's third largest

236 D. Treisman. 2010. 'Oil and Democracy In Russia', National Bureau for Economic Research Working Paper 15667. Available at: www.nber.org/papers/w15667 [Accessed April 2014].

237 W. Kononczuk. 2012. *Russia's Best Ally: The Situation of the Russian Oil Sector and Forecasts for its Future*, Centre for Eastern Studies. Available at: http://www.osw.waw.pl/en/eksperci/wojciech-kononczuk [Accessed April 2014].

producer.[238] In 2005, Rosneft bought 10.74 per cent of Gazprom to take the level of state ownership in the company to 50 per cent. In 2006, Gazprom paid US$13.7 billion to buy out private interests in Sibfnet (led by Abramovich) and renamed the company Gazpromneft.

Oil is the lifeblood of the Russian economy. Kononczuk (2012) has the following to say: 'Income generated by oil sales have been the basis for the stabilisation of the socio-economic situation in Russia since 2000. This, in turn, is one of the key factors that adds legitimacy to the governments of the country, and ensures a high level of public support for the political elite led by Vladimir Putin ... oil is also a foreign policy instrument'.[239] Although Putin has correctly sought to capture a higher share of hydrocarbon rents, the country has failed to diversify its economy away from oil, which the elites acknowledge. 'One hundred and forty dollars per barrel would be a catastrophe; it would destroy all incentives for development,' Putin has said.[240]

NORWAY

Norway, with a population of nearly 5 million people, and a GDP per capita of almost US$100,000, is a US$500 billion economy.[241] It is the world's fourth richest country, according to the World Bank.[242] The country is not a member of the European Union (EU) or the Eurozone. In 2012, Norway was the world's 14th largest oil producer and was Europe's second largest producer (after Russia) with production of 1.9 million bpd. This was equivalent to 2.1 per cent of world production and 13.8 per cent of European production. In 2012, Norway was the world's sixth largest producer of natural gas and Europe's second largest producer (after Russia) with production of 114.9 billion cubic metres. This was equivalent to 3.4 per cent of world production and 13.2 per cent of European production. In the same year, the petroleum sector contributed 23 per cent to the country's GDP, 30 per cent of state revenues, 29 per cent of total investment and 52 per cent of total exports.[243]

Norway's hydrocarbons extractive regime has an aggressive government take system through high levels of tax and state ownership. In addition to the normal 28 per cent tax rate, which applies to all companies, there is a 50 per

238　J. Henderson. 2012. 'Rosneft – On the Road to Global NOC Status?' Oxford Institute for Energy Studies. Available at: www.oxfordenergy.org/wpcms/wp-content/.../2012/01/WPM_44.pdf [Accessed April 2014].

239　W. Kononczuk. 2012. *Russia's Best Ally: The Situation of the Russian Oil Sector and Forecasts for its Future*, Centre for Eastern Studies. Available at: http://www.osw.waw.pl/en/eksperci/wojciech-kononczuk [Accessed April 2014].

240　W. Kononczuk. 2012. *Russia's Best Ally: The Situation of the Russian Oil Sector and Forecasts for its Future*, Centre for Eastern Studies. Available at: http://www.osw.waw.pl/en/eksperci/wojciech-kononczuk [Accessed April 2014].

241　The statistics in this section are obtained from the Appendices to this report where sources are provided. Refer to Table 1.

242　World Development Indicators Database: http://data.worldbank.org/indicator/NY.GDP.PCAP.CD [Accessed April 2014].

243　The statistics in this section are obtained from the Appendices to this report where sources are provided. Refer to Tables 7–13.

cent profit tax for the petroleum sector. Therefore, the government receives 78 per cent of the profits of petroleum companies. There are other minor taxes such as carbon dioxide and area fees.[244] The government owns the State Direct Financial Interest (SDFI), which has a portfolio of mostly minority and passive stakes in 158 production licences and 15 joint ventures for pipelines and onshore facilities. The SDFI's portfolio was valued at US$190 billion in January 2012.[245] The government also owns a 67 per cent shareholding in listed Statoil, the National Oil Company (NOC), which was worth US$65 billion at the end of April 2014. Statoil, with revenues of US$105 billion in 2013, has 23,000 employees working in 33 countries and territories. Acting as an operator, the company is responsible for 69 per cent of all oil and gas production on the Norwegian continental shelf (NCF).[246] If one adds the attributable production from Statoil's partner-operated fields and the SDFI portfolio, it becomes clear that the state's share of production is very high. According to one estimate, the state collects nearly 90 per cent of the country's petroleum rent.[247]

Norway accumulates the revenues from its government take system in the Government Pension Fund Global (GPFG), whose portfolio was worth US$830 billion at the end of December 2013.[248] Therefore, Norway has accumulated assets worth US$1.1 trillion, comprising commercial interests in the Norwegian oil sector worth US$255 billion and the GPFG's offshore investments worth US$830 billion. In 2011, the net cash flow to the state from petroleum activities was 355.1 billion Norwegian Kroner (NOK), equivalent to US$63.3 billion. This comprised taxes of NOK214.7 billion (US$38.2 billion), net income from the SDFI of NOK122.7 billion (US$21.9 billion) and Statoil dividends of NOK13.9 billion (US$2.5 billion).[249]

The Norwegian model includes a clear separation of the government's political, regulatory and commercial functions. The Ministry of Petroleum and Energy is responsible for the political and policy functions. The National Petroleum Directorate (NPD) is a professional body that is responsible for the regulatory and administrative functions and the overall management of the sector. Statoil and SDFI are responsible for the commercial functions. The model also has a

244 Norwegian Petroleum Directorate, 'Facts 2013: The Norwegian Petroleum Sector'. Available at: http://npd.no/en/Publications/Facts/Facts-2013/ [Accessed April 2014].

245 Ministry of Petroleum and Energy website: http://www.regjeringen.no/en/dep/oed/Subject/state-participation-in-the-petroleum-sec/the-states-direct-financial-interest-sdf.html?id=445748 [Accessed April 2014].

246 *Statoil Annual Report 2013*: http://www.statoil.com/en/investorcentre/annualreport/annualreport2013/pages/default.aspx [Accessed April 2014].

247 A. Cappelen and L. Mjoset. 2009. 'Can Norway be a Role Model for Natural Resource Abundant Countries?' United Nations University-World Institute for Development Economics Research (UNU-Wider). Available at: www.wider.unu.edu/publications/.../2009/en.../rp2009.../RP2009-23.pdf [Accessed May 2014].

248 *Government Pension Fund Global 2013 Annual Report and Presentation*, Norges Bank Investment Management website :http://www.nbim.no/en/transparency/reports/2013/annual-report/ [Accessed May 2014].

249 Royal Ministry of Finance, 'The National Budget 2014: A Summary', Ministry of Finance website: http://www.regjeringen.no/en/dep/fin/Selected-topics/the-national-budget.html?id=1437 [Accessed May 2014].

clear distinction between the active (or operational) investment functions of Statoil and the passive investment functions of the SDFI.[250] The government established a professional agency called Petoro to manage the SDFI's portfolio of assets. The Norwegian Central Bank (Norges Bank) manages the GPFG through a professional entity called Norges Bank Investment Management (NBIM).[251]

In 2001, Norway introduced a fiscal rule to guide the spending of oil revenues. According to the government: 'The fiscal rule specifies that transfers from the fund to the central government shall, over time, reflect the expected real return on the fund, which is estimated at 4 per cent of the fund's capital at the beginning of the year.' Therefore, the GPFG operates like an endowment. It takes all the country's net petroleum revenues each year (taxes, returns from the SDFI and dividends from Statoil minus the costs of managing these petroleum activities) and the returns from the fund (interest, dividends and increases in the values of its investments). But the country can only spend, over time, 4 per cent of the value of the fund. Since the fund grows each year, the actual value of the 4 per cent also grows. In practice, this means that the government's budget can have a non-oil structural deficit (after correcting for cyclical changes of spending and revenue) that is equal to the 4 per cent return.[252]

According to economic historian Ryggvik (2010), Norway's modern industrial revolution at the beginning of the twentieth century was based on the exploitation of cheap waterpower (today the waterfalls provide most of the country's electricity). Like many countries in the Global South today, Norway had neither the capital nor the technology to exploit this resource. The big question was how to use foreign interests without losing control over development. It was decided that 'the energy of Norwegian waterfalls had been given by nature. Its value should not go to any individuals'.[253] The new waterfall laws determined that the energy, and hence the value, which could be collected from the waterfalls belonged to the state. This was a radical encroachment on forest owners and large farmers, who often owned the wood and land on both sides of the river banks. The concessions regime provided foreign capital with the space to exploit the resources while the state acquired the know-how to do so itself. 'When the oil companies came to Norway in the 1960s, the

250 R. Gordon and T. Stenvoll. 2007. 'Statoil: A Study In Political Entrepreneurship', James Baker III Institute For Public Policy, Rice University. Available at: http://bakerinstitute.org/files/2480/ [Accessed May 2014].

251 Norwegian Petroleum Directorate, 'Facts 2013: The Norwegian Petroleum Sector'. Available at: http://npd.no/en/Publications/ Facts/Facts-2013/ [Accessed April 2014].

252 Royal Ministry of Finance, 'The National Budget 2014: A Summary', Ministry of Finance website: http://www.regjeringen.no/en/ dep/fin/Selected-topics/the-national-budget.html?id=1437 [Accessed April 2014].

253 H. Ryggvik. 2010. 'The Norwegian Oil Experience: A Toolbox for Managing Resources?' Centre for technology Innovation and Culture. Available at: http://www.google.co.za/ url?sa=t&rct=j&q=&esrc=s&source=web&cd=1&ved=0CCcQFjAA&url=http%3A%2F%2Fwww.sv.uio.no%2Ftik%2Fforskning% 2Fpublikasjoner%2Ftik-artikkelserie%2FRyggvik.pdf&ei= billionVjU5j3A4LT7Aadu4C4Bg&usg=AFQjCNEODrygrTm39dRVD9ng rE-m3zJw9A&bvm=bv.65788261,d.ZGU&cad=rja [Accessed April 2014].

vast majority of water power production was publicly owned and operated. It was, therefore, entirely natural that the allocation of rights for prospecting and potential extraction of oil and gas conformed to the legal approach and ideology, which were already built into the existing Norwegian concessions regime,' Ryggvik says.[254]

Once oil had been discovered, Norway was in a better bargaining position.[255] Ryggvik says the initial oil policies had been shaped by a small group of civil servants. It later involved all layers of society. Between 1971 and 1973, the country had four governments, and each change of government represented a move to the left. Then there was the international oil crisis. In this environment there were extensive debates in parliament and civil society. 'In the first half of the 1970s, an almost overwhelming stream of reports, white papers and committees were developed, covering all sorts of challenges linked to oil activities. These committees drew on the general expertise that was available in professional institutions,' Ryggvik recalls.[256]

One document stands out for outlining the future direction of oil policy. The parliament's extended industrial committee produced a report in 1971 that outlined ten points ('The 10 Oil Commandments') to ensure that natural resources are exploited in a way that benefits the whole society:

1. National governance and control must be secured for all activities on the NCF.
2. Norway must become independent of others in the supply of crude oil.
3. A new industrial sector should be developed, based on petroleum.
4. This development must take existing business activities and environmental protection into consideration as necessary.
5. Usable gas should not be burnt off.
6. Petroleum deposits should be brought ashore in Norway, as a general rule.
7. The state must be involved at all appropriate levels and contribute to a coordination of Norwegian interests in Norway's petroleum industry as well as the creation of an integrated oil community, which sets its sights both nationally and internationally.
8. A state oil company will be established which can look after the government's interests and pursue appropriate collaboration with domestic and foreign oil interests.

---

254 Ibid.

255 J. Moses. 2010. *Foiling the Resource Curse: Wealth, Equality, Oil and the Norwegian State in Constructing a Democratic Developmental State in South Africa* (ed. Omano Edigheji), HSRC Press.

256 H. Ryggvik. 2010. 'The Norwegian Oil Experience: A Toolbox for Managing Resources?' Centre for Technology Innovation and Culture. Available at: http://www.google.co.za/url?sa=t&rct=j&q=&esrc=s&source=web&cd=1&ved=0CCcQFjAA&url=http%3A%2F%2Fwww.sv.uio.no%2Ftik%2Fforskning%2Fpublikasjoner%2Ftik-artikkelserie%2FRyggvik.pdf&ei= billionVjU5j3A4LT7Aadu4C4Bg&usg=AFQjCNEODrygrTm39dRVD9ng rE-m3zJw9A&bvm=bv.65788261,d.ZGU&cad=rja [Accessed April 2014].

9. A pattern of activities must be selected north of the 62nd parallel which reflects the socio-political conditions prevailing in that part of the country.
10. Large Norwegian petroleum discoveries could present new tasks for Norway's foreign policy.

Later, a white paper said the wealth from oil should be used to create a qualitatively better society. 'Wishing for a long-term perspective in the exploitation of resources, and after a comprehensive evaluation of its social aspects, the government has concluded that Norway should take a moderate pace in the extraction of petroleum resources.'[257] In another report, the Ministry of Finance said: 'Democratically elected institutions must have full control of all important aspects of petroleum policy.'[258] Ryggvik (2010) says the documents expressed a widespread understanding that it would not be enough simply to tax foreign companies if Norway was to see a benefit from the new industry. 'Norway also had to secure the greatest possible share of the wealth creation that would take place around the industrial side of oil activities.'

Eventually, the state, through its various control instruments, came to own as much as 80 per cent of all the operations on the Shelf. Subsequent concession rounds began to include non-economic or technical conditions that secured a broader Norwegian contribution and became the core of a new industrial policy. 'For example, in 1972, the Ministry of Industry established a Goods and Service Office that monitored the contracting and procurement process to ensure that qualified Norwegian firms were on various tender lists and that bids had a sufficiently large Norwegian content, measured in personnel and monetary terms. In addition, the government imposed a number for knowledge transfers requirements,' Moses (2010) says.[259]

The Norwegian model, Moses (ibid) notes, has developed a system that combines effective and professional management with democratic control. This tricky blend of objectives is secured by steeping political decisions in institutional frameworks that encourage participants to think beyond their own parochial interests. Although there appear to be few controversies around this model in Norway, there are some concerns. There is a view, expressed by Ryggvik (2010), that there has been a dilution of democratic control as a new oil-industrial complex pursues its own interests of internationalisation, which require it to break free from political oversight.

257 Ryggvik, H. 2010. 'The Norwegian Oil Experience: A Toolbox for Managing Resources?' Centre for Technology Innovation and Culture. Available at: http://www.google.co.za/url?sa=t&rct=j&q=&esrc=s&source=web&cd=1&ved=0CCcQFjAA&url=http%3A%2F%2Fwww.sv.uio.no%2Ftik%2Fforskning%2Fpublikasjoner%2Ftik-artikkelserie%2FRyggvik.pdf&ei= billionVjU5j3A4LT7Aadu4C4Bg&usg=AFQjCNEODrygrTm39dRVD9ngrE-m3zJw9A&bvm=bv.65788261,d.ZGU&cad=rja [Accessed 10 April 2014].

258 Moses, J. 2010. *Foiling the Resource Curse: Wealth, Equality, Oil and the Norwegian State in Constructing a Democratic Developmental State in South Africa* (ed. Omano Edigheji), HSRC Press.

259 H. Ryggvik. 2010. 'The Norwegian Oil Experience: A Toolbox for Managing Resources?' Centre for Technology Innovation and Culture.

If a depoliticised Statoil is to be managed on the basis of profit and the interests of the 30 per cent shareholders on the stock exchanges, it might have to shut down marginal fields, even though they could continue to produce at a profit. There are also concerns about the intense rate of extraction. The country comes close to holding the world record for high-speed production. This has driven the rapid increase of assets within the GPFG. A slower pace of extraction could have delivered a better return in the long-run because the oil price has performed much better than the rich countries in which the GPFG is invested. It could be argued that this situation could continue in the future.[260] The GPFG's investment policy has come under scrutiny and been criticised for an excessive focus on developed countries with low economic growth prospects as opposed to developing countries.[261] There have been calls for the fund's climate change policy to ban investments in coal, oil and gas companies. The government has appointed a committee to review such investments.

UNITED KINGDOM

The United Kingdom (UK), with a population of 62.6 million and a GDP per capita of US$38 514, is a US$2.5 trillion economy, the third largest in Europe and the sixth largest in the world.[262] In 2012, the oil and gas sector contributed 1.6 per cent to the country's GDP.[263] The industry provides employment for more than 400,000 people, of whom 45 per cent are in Scotland. In 2012, the industry invested £11.5 billion (US$18.7 billion), the highest for all sectors in the economy. In 2012/13 the industry paid £6.5 billion in corporate taxes, equivalent to 15 per cent of all company taxes.[264] According to the Wood Review (2014), the first licences for the extraction of oil and gas from the UK Continental Shelf (UKCS) were issued in 1964. Over the last 50 years, the industry has invested £500 billion (in 2012 money) in exploration, development and production activities. To date, the UK Treasury has received more than £300 billion in production taxes.[265]

The oil and gas industry has experienced an alarming decline in production over the past decade. This has invited unflattering comparisons with Norway,

260 http://www.google.co.za/url?sa=t&rct=j&q=&esrc=s&source=web&cd=1&ved=0CCcQFjAA&url=http%3A%2F%2Fwww.sv.uio.no%2Ftik%2Fforskning%2Fpublikasjoner%2Ftik-artikkelserie%2FRyggvik.pdf&ei=billionVjU5j3A4LT7Aadu4C4Bg&usg=AFQjCNEODrygrTm39dRVD9ngrE-m3zJw9A&bvm=bv.65788261,d.ZGU&cad=rja [Accessed April 2014].

261 Kapoor, S. 2013. 'Investing for the Future: Good for Norway – Good for Development', Redefine and Norwegian Church Aid Act Alliance. Available at: www.re-define.org/sites/default/.../ReDefineReportonNorwaySWF.pdf [Accessed May 2014].

262 The statistics in this section are obtained from the Appendices to this report where sources are provided. Refer to Table 1.

263 The Department of Energy and Climate Change. 2013. 'UK Energy In Brief 2013': https://www.gov.uk/government/.../uk_energy_in_brief_2013.PDF [Accessed May 2014].

264 Wood, I. 2014. 'UKCS Maximising Recovery Review: Final Report'. Available at http://www.woodreview.co.uk/ [Accessed May 2014].

265 Ibid.

the country's northern neighbour. According to the Scottish Government: 'In 1970, levels of GDP per capita in Norway were 8.9 per cent lower than in the UK. By 2011, GDP per capita in Norway was 71.5 per cent higher than in the UK.'[266] The two countries discovered oil at roughly the same time and in the same ocean. For the first two decades, during the 1960s and 1970s, they implemented similar policies for the oil industry. Although the timing of extraction and the prices received for oil were different, the two countries have both emptied some 3,400 tonnes of oil from the icy waters of the North Sea over the past 40 years.

Recently, Aditya Chakrobortty wrote in the British *The Guardian* newspaper: 'Our oil cash was magicked into tax cuts for the well-off, then micturated against the walls of a thousand pricey car dealerships and estate agents.' He cited research by John Hawksworth, an economist from Price Waterhouse, who estimated that if the UK had invested half of its oil revenues in a sovereign wealth fund, it would have accumulated assets of £450 billion by 2008.[267] The mismanagement of the UK's oil and gas wealth, and the lack of benefits that have accrued to the people of Scotland, is one of the key messages of the campaign led by the ruling Scottish National Party (SNP) for a 'Yes' vote in a referendum on independence which was held on 13 September 2014. According to one estimate, 96 per cent of oil production and 52 per cent of gas production in 2011 was from Scotland's geographic share of the UKCS. The Scottish government's strategy for the sector has called for an independent Scotland to establish a short-term stabilisation fund and a long-term savings fund.[268]

The extractive regime for the hydrocarbons sector is based on high taxes and 'light touch' regulation. There has been no state participation in the industry since the privatisations of the 1980s. According to the Scottish government, the UK's oil and gas fiscal regime (which was introduced in 2011) has three elements. The petroleum revenue tax (PRT) is levied at 50 per cent of profits from oil and gas fields that were given development approval prior to March 1993. The tax is levied on a per field basis and not on a company's UKCS operations as a whole. The corporation tax is charged at 30 per cent on profits net of the PRT. The supplementary charge is charged at 32 per cent and acts as an effective increase in the corporation tax rate. Therefore, the marginal tax rate on fields approved before 1993 is 81 per cent. Fields approved after this

266 The Scottish Government. 2013. 'Maximising the Return from Oil and Gas in an Independent Scotland'. Available at www.scotland.gov.uk/Resource/0042/00428074.pdf [Accessed May 2013].

267 Aditya Chakrabortty. 2014. 'Dude, Where is my Oil Money?' *The Guardian*, 13 January.

268 The Scottish Government. 2013. 'Maximising the Return from Oil and Gas in an Independent Scotland'. Available at: www.scotland.gov.uk/Resource/0042/00428074.pdf [Accessed May 2013].
     The Scottish Government. 2013. 'Fiscal Commisssion Working Group Stabilisation and Savings Funds for Scotland'. Available at: www.scotland.gov.uk/Resource/0043/00435303.pdf [Accessed May 2014].

date have a marginal tax rate of 62 per cent.[269] Before the tax changes, the rates were 75 per cent for fields approved before 1993 and 50 per cent for fields approved after this date.

The latest US Energy Information Administration (EIA) country analysis brief for the UK says that projects have become less competitive as a result of the significant increases in taxes. 'Increases in operating costs coupled with higher taxes have decreased investment in both brownfields and new exploration. Even without the increased taxes, operating costs of the UKCS were prohibitively high, exacerbated by the high decommissioning costs of old facilities, which also discourage investors. Almost immediately after the new taxes were implemented, development on several start-ups was suspended, including Statoil's Mariner and Chevron's Bressay fields. Centrica launched a review of all its exploration activities. Given a nearly 16 per cent decline in production following the implementation of the new tax rates, the government has introduced new incentives for producers.'

The Wood Review of the industry (2014), commissioned by the government, says the system of 'light touch' regulation is in need of a major overhaul to create a new regulator that can reverse the massive decline of production over the past decade. 'The present regulator has halved in size over the last 20 years and, as a result, is clearly struggling to perform a more demanding stewardship role. The problems the review has identified will be largely resolved by evolving the model to introduce a stronger regulator with broader skills and capabilities able to significantly enhance the level of coordination and collaboration. The new regulator's role will be licensing, supervision and stewardship. It will play a vital role in facilitating, coordinating, mediating, promoting and catalysing collaboration, removing barriers, and encouraging more efficient exploration, development and production.'[270]

After the discovery of natural gas in The Netherlands in 1959, IOCs became more interested in exploring for oil and gas in the North Sea. During the 1960s, the UK reached agreement with Norway and Denmark on the demarcation of the North Sea. The next step was to develop a licensing system. During the 1960s, the UK, like Norway, implemented a licensing system that incorporated a minimum of state intervention. According to one account, in 1964, the conservative government gave away 40 per cent of the UK sector of the North Sea, the richest area, with no conditions. State-controlled British Petroleum got its fair share. But the lion's share went to Shell Esso. The context changed during the early 1970s due to the discovery of large fields in the UK (Forties

269 The Scottish Government. 2013. 'Fiscal Commission Working Group Stabilisation and Savings Funds for Scotland'. Available at: www.scotland.gov.uk/Resource/0043/00435303.pdf [Accessed May 2014].

270 I. Wood. 2014. 'UKCS Maximising Recovery Review: Final Report'. Available at: http://www.woodreview.co.uk/ [Accessed May 2014].

discovered by BP in 1970) and Norway (Ekofisk discovered by Phillips in 1969), events in the Middle East that shifted power to producer nations, and the election of a labour government with a commitment to state ownership. According to Nelsen (1992), the UK did not transform its liberal offshore licensing system until after Norway. But the result was a similar shift from minimal state intervention on the UK shelf towards state participation in the oil industry.

The centrepiece of Labour's offshore programme was the BILLIONOC, which parliament created in 1975 to manage the state's share of offshore licences. Following on the Norwegian model, officials gave BNOC the right to 51 per cent of every new licence on a 'carried interest' basis. The government also negotiated with IOCs a series of participation agreements that gave BILLIONOC the formal title to 51 per cent of all existing licences covering more than 800 blocks. In reality, these agreements gave BILLIONOC the right to 51 per cent of the petroleum produced on the shelf, plus a seat and a vote (but not a veto) on the operating committees of the North Sea consortia. BILLIONOC became a major European oil trader and offshore operator after 1976. After settling the issue of state participation, the Department of Energy (DOE) proceeded to strengthen its control of offshore activities. The fifth licensing round in 1977 mimicked the terms offered in Norway and reflected a harder line. BILLIONOC was appointed as the operator in several blocks and awarded licences in a special round that was not open to private companies. The government introduced a new PRT to capture the benefits of rising oil prices. In line with the Norwegian model, the UK set up an offshore supplies office (OSO) to push IOCs to buy British goods and services.

The election of Thatcher as Prime Minister in 1979 changed the course of the industry. She had a mandate to restructure the economy through free market reforms and privatisation. The government ended the state's entrepreneurial activities on the UKCS through the sale of its offshore interests, the most lucrative of which were parcelled into a company called Britoil. The new company was privatised in November 1982. British Petroleum, which had established a strong presence in Iran and the rest of the Middle East under state ownership, was sold in stages. In June 1977, under the labour government, the state shareholding was reduced to 51 per cent from 68 per cent. Under Thatcher, there were further sales of state shares in 1979, 1983 and 1987, when the company was listed. In 1986, British Gas was privatised in a successful initial public offering, which raised £9 billion.

The UK's oil and gas sector now faces an uncertain future after a decade of rapid decline. According to the Wood Review, the structure of the industry has changed. During the 1970s and 1980s the industry attracted IOCs. A small number of large fields dominated production, but today's production comes from more than 300 fields operated by a diverse mix of companies who are far more independent than before. Most new fields are much smaller in size. The UKCS is now one of the most mature offshore basins in the world, but there are still some interesting frontier areas, exploration plays, and huge opportunities in maximising brownfield recovery. The review says production has fallen by 38 per cent over the past three years, with the Shelf producing about 500 million barrels of oil equivalent (mboe) less over the period, 360 million of which is due to the rapid fall in production efficiency, which has cost the national treasury £6 billion in lower tax receipts. Exploration is at an all-time low and some operating assets are more than 30 years old – at or beyond the end of their design life. The industry has been criticised for not making full use of technology, and cost pressures are also a significant challenge, with the Shelf being on one of the more expensive basins in the world.

The Wood Review says that the industry has already produced 42 billion barrels of oil equivalent (boe). It estimates that a further 12 to 24 billion boe could be produced with ultimate recovery in a large part dependent on how well the UK manages its remaining resources. The review makes a number of recommendations to arrest the industry's decline: 'At the very low end, if implemented fully and quickly, the recommendations have the potential to deliver 3–4 billion boe over the next 20 years, worth about £200 billion at today's prices.' The Scottish government cites a report by PWC, which says that it is likely that there is between 24 and 30 billion boe still to gather from the North Sea. 'Analysis by the Scottish government suggests that the 24 billion boe of reserves have a potential wholesale value of £1.5 trillion – 10 times the size of the Scottish economy. This indicates that more than half of the oil and gas reserves in the UKCS, by value, still have to be extracted.'[271] Whatever the number, it remains to be seen what model the UK will use to maximise benefits for its citizens.

CONCLUSION

According to this chapter, Europe comprises 45 countries, has a population of 739 million and a combined GDP of US$20.2 billion in 2012, equivalent to 28.2 per cent of the world's total output.[272] Most European countries have relatively high living standards (26 are advanced economies, according to the IMF) after almost two centuries of steady increases in GDP per capita. For most countries (excluding Russia), non-renewable natural resources (energy

271 I. Wood. 2014. 'UKCS Maximising Recovery Review: Final Report'. Available at: http://www.woodreview.co.uk/documents/ UKCS%20Maximising%20Recovery%20Review%20FINAL%2072pp%20locked.pdf [Accessed May 2014].

272 The statistics in this section are obtained from the Appendices to this report where sources are provided. Refer to Table 1.

and metallic minerals) have not played a major role in the development of their economies, especially during the last century, when Europe's role as a centre of global mining diminished rapidly. Russia, which accounts for 68 per cent of Europe's land area, is a major producer of energy and metallic minerals. Most of the energy and metallic minerals in Europe are located in Russia.

The case studies in this chapter have looked at Russia, Norway and the UK (oil and gas producers), and producers of renewable natural resources (forests and forest-related products). A review of international best practices in harnessing mineral resources for economic growth and development identified seven key issues in non-renewable natural resource governance.[273] **Firstly, a strategy for mineral resources must be located within a national vision and strategy for economic growth and development, which has the support of key stakeholders.** There are many drivers of economic growth and development, many of which are beyond the scope of this report. Therefore, it is a challenge to isolate the impact of natural resource policies on the economy. In this regard, two issues are critical: the overall policy stance and the size of the relevant natural resource sector/s as a percentage of GDP and exports. However, it appears that getting the right macro-economic policies matters more than the presence (or lack) of natural resources.

Norway and the UK had robust economic growth during the 'Golden Era' (1950–1973), when they pursued Keynesian policies aimed at achieving rapid economic growth and full employment. The three countries had tripartite social contracts between state, capital and labour, which managed macro-economic policy during the Bretton Woods era of fixed exchange rates. There were frequent devaluations to restore the competitiveness of export industries. This required the support of trade unions to implement incomes policies that moderated wage increases to prevent inflationary spirals following devaluation. This 'Golden Era' was followed by lower rates of GDP per capita growth during the 'Neo-Liberal Order' (1973–2008), when the focus of policy-makers changed towards price stability.[274]

Norway's GDP per capita growth rate was 3.19 per cent during the first period and 2.67 per cent during the second period. The country underperformed against the Western European average (4.05 per cent) during the first period. But Norway had a higher GDP per capita growth rate than the Western European average (1.93 per cent) during the second period, which allowed it to overtake many countries in terms of GDP per capita levels. Although Norway had a better relative performance than Western Europe during the 'Neo-liberal

---

273 Kio Advisory Services. 2010. 'Harnessing South Africa's Mineral Resources for Economic Growth and Development: Lessons and Experiences From Abroad', South African Mining Development Association.
274 A. Maddison. 2006. *The World Economy*, OECD.

Order', it had a lower GDP per capita growth rate after it had discovered oil and gas when compared with the first period.[275]

The UK's GDP per capita growth rate was 2.42 per cent during the first period and 1.96 per cent during the second period. The country significantly underperformed against the Western European average during the first period. It was in line with the Western European average during the second period. But, like Norway, the UK had a lower GDP per capita growth rate after it had discovered oil and gas when compared with the first period. However, the oil and gas sector has far less weight in the UK's economy than in Norway. This is because Norway has a smaller economy and population.

The second key issue in harnessing mineral resources for economic growth and development is to **develop a national vision and plan for non-renewable natural resources.** The best example is Norway's '10 Oil Commandments' – a set of instructions given to the government by parliament for the development of the country's petroleum sector. The key principles included national management and control of all activities on the Norwegian continental shelf and state involvement at all levels to protect national interests and to ensure the development of a Norwegian industrial oil cluster.

Thirdly, countries must **develop the state capacity to lead the sector.** State capacity is the initiator of economic growth and development. It determines whether a resource endowment will be a curse or a blessing. The best-practice model of organisation of the sector is in Norway, where there is a clear separation between the government's policy, regulatory and commercial functions. Norway and Russia have established professional agencies for regulation, administration and overall management of the industry. Russia splits the regulatory and administrative functions into two agencies responsible for licensing and approving development plans and monitoring compliance. The UK has acknowledged the weaknesses of its 'light touch' regulation and is setting up a new regulator to help reverse the industry's decline. In terms of managing the commercial functions, the Norwegian model has a clear distinction between the active (or operational) investment functions of Statoil and the passive investment functions of the SDFI.

Fourthly, the state must develop measures – a government 'take system' — to extract a fair share of natural resource rents. In between the false dichotomies of nationalisation and privatisation, there are as many ways of slicing the rent as there are countries in the world. Each model is unique. The models involve various combinations of state equity, state-owned companies, tax regimes

---

275 Ibid.

(windfall and resource rent taxes and royalties) and contract types (production sharing agreements, joint ventures and concessions.) Norway has the most aggressive government take system, which collects nearly 90 per cent of the country's petroleum rent.[276] It includes 67 per cent state ownership of Statoil, ownership of the SDFI and a 78 per cent tax rate. The state shareholdings in Statoil and the SDFI are worth about US$255 billion.

Russia has two national champions. Rosneft, with 69.5 per cent state ownership, has a market capitalisation of US$60 billion and controls 40 per cent of national oil production.[277] Total state control, after taking into account state ownership in other producers, is 46 per cent.[278] Gazprom, with 50 per cent state ownership, has a market capitalisation of US$85 billion and controls 74 per cent of national natural gas production.[279] The tax regime takes more than 70 per cent of petroleum revenues at current oil prices. The UK has no state ownership and relatively high taxes – 81 per cent tax for fields approved before 1993 and 62 per cent for fields approved after this date.

Fifthly, there are two challenges in managing natural resource rents: the volatility of commodity prices and Dutch Disease, whereby a resource boom can result in the appreciation of the currency and the loss of competitiveness of other traded sectors of the economy. Countries have used sovereign wealth and stabilisation funds to cream off excess commodity revenues and smooth expenditure to avoid boom and bust cycles. Norway has a sovereign wealth fund that had assets worth US$830 billion at the end of December 2013. The example of the UK shows that it is not enough to just tax natural resources to extract benefits for the population. The UK Treasury received more than £300 billion in taxes over the past four decades, but has nothing to show, except a rapidly declining oil industry. According to one study, the country would have had a fund worth £450 billion in 2008 if it had invested half of its oil revenues. Russia has two funds. The Reserve Fund, which had assets of US$84.7 billion in February 2013, has a mandate to stabilise fiscal revenues and finance the budget deficit. The National Wealth Fund, which had assets of US$86.7 billion in February 2013, has a mandate to support the country's national pension fund.

Norway and the UK appear to have avoided a full-blown Dutch Disease, although they may have shown mild symptoms of it at times. In the former USSR, the stagnation of the economy from the early 1970s coincided with the

---

276 A. Cappelen and L. Mjoset. 2009. 'Can Norway be a Role Model for Natural Resource Abundant Countries?' United Nations University-World Institute for Development Economics Research (UNU-Wider). Available at: www.wider.unu.edu/ publications/.../2009/en.../rp2009.../RP2009-23.pdf [Accessed May 2014].

277 Rosneft website: www.rosneft.com [Accessed May 2014].

278 The statistics in this section are obtained from the Appendices to this report where sources are provided. Refer to Table 49.

279 Gazprom website: www.gazprom.com [Accessed May 2014].

country becoming a major producer of oil. This suggests that it is a case study of the natural resource (or Siberian) curse. According to Iyoha and Oriakhi (2002), 'the "natural resource curse" goes beyond standard "Dutch disease" effects and may involve a general de-emphasis of growth-orientated economic activities such as agriculture and manufacturing when the contribution of a specific natural resource seems to meet current expenditure requirements.'[280] As the former USSR earned more petrodollars (it became the world's largest producer in 1975), its trade deficits increased as imports of grain and consumer goods increased faster than the soaring oil exports.

Sixthly, countries must invest the natural resource rents wisely – in infrastructure, technology, human capital and diversifying the economy. According to Stiglitz (2005), since extraction makes a country poorer, it is the subsequent re-investment in capital that can offset the depletion of natural resources and make a country richer.[281] Countries can invest their natural resource rents in a number of ways. They can accumulate financial assets, invest in infrastructure and human capital, fund public consumption, fund private consumption, return some of the revenues to citizens, or invest in activities that will diversify the economy. Initially, Norway funded public consumption as it invested in its welfare state. Later, it accumulated financial assets. The UK blew the oil windfall on tax cuts. Russia's stabilisation fund was used as a tool for counter-cyclical fiscal policy and invested US$100 billion in the economy in the aftermath of the Great Recession.

However, there is a big difference between having a 'rainy day' fund to smooth fiscal revenues and accumulating for the sake of it. Countries seeking to emulate Norway should consider that it was not until the early 2000s that its sovereign wealth fund started expanding. During the previous 30 years, the country made massive investments in social welfare. Also, Yevgeny Primakov, a former prime minister of Russia, has opposed the 'Fetishisation of the Stabilisation Fund – Our beloved Piggy Bank' – and argued that it should be spent on primary needs to buy tangible capital goods.[282] Although developing countries should learn from Norway's institutions, policies and tools to extract natural resource rents, few will ever be able to justify to their electorates the excessive accumulation of foreign financial assets in the face of massive domestic infrastructure and human capital backlogs.

---

280   M. Iyoha and D. Oriakhi. 2002. *Explaining African Economic Growth Performance: The Case of Nigeria in Economic Growth in Africa* (eds. B. Ndulu, et al.). Cambridge University Press.

281   J. Stiglitz. 2005. 'Making Natural Resources a Blessing Rather than a Curse' in A. Schiffin and S. Tsalik (eds.) *Covering Oil: A Reporters Guide to Energy Development*, Open Society Institute. Available at: http://www.opensocietyfoundations.org/sites/default/files/osicoveringoil_20050803.pdf [Accessed May 2014].

282   M. Hudson. 'Taming the Speculators: What should Countries do with Their Central Bank Reserves?' *Global Research*, 14 May 2009. Available at: www.globalresearch.ca/taming-the-speculators-what...do.../13616 [Accessed May 2013].
      M. Hudson. 2011. 'What Does Norway Get Out of its Oil Fund, if not More Strategic Infrastructure Investment?', Levy Economic Institute of Bard College Working Paper 657. Available at http://papers.ssrn.com/sol3/papers.cfm?abstract_id=1785668 [Accessed May 2014].

Resurgent Resource Nationalism? A Study Into The Global Phenomenon | Europe

101

Norway's example is one of extreme fiscal prudence, which is probably not appropriate for Norwegians, even if one takes into account their country's high level of economic development. The country's GDP per capita growth has declined during the post-oil era when compared with the 'Golden Era' from 1950 to 1973. Hudson (2011) says the country should rather focus on developing its own economy and diversifying it away from oil. The neo-liberal fear of inflation explains the excessive accumulation of foreign financial assets. But this assumes that all government spending is inflationary and cannot generate the production to absorb it, he notes.[283]

Finally, natural resource projects tend to be capital-intensive enclaves with few linkages with the rest of the economy. **According to the Africa Mining Vision, there is a need (in South Africa) to diversify the economy through: downstream linkages (beneficiation and manufacturing), upstream linkages (mining capital goods, consumables and services industries), and side-stream linkages into infrastructure and skills and technology development.**[284] Hence, many countries implement local content policies to create these linkages.[285]

Norway implemented local procurement requirements during earlier licensing rounds and established a Goods and Services Office to steer purchases by oil companies towards Norwegian companies. As a result, the country now has a developed domestic industrial cluster that services the oil and gas industry. In the UK, the government increased levels of state ownership during the 1970s and established an Offshore Supplies Office (OSO) to encourage IOCs to buy British goods and services. However, Russia has made little progress in diversifying its economy away from oil. According to Kononczuk (2012), 'An increase in the oil price of 10 per cent translates into 0.9 per cent GDP growth, at most. An increase (or decrease) in oil prices by US$2 a barrel automatically makes the state budget revenues go up (or down) by US$3 billion.'

283 Ibid.

284 Africa Mining Vision. Available at: http://www.africaminingvision.org/ [Accessed May 2014].

285 Kio Advisory Services. 2010. 'Harnessing South Africa's Mineral Resources for Economic Growth and Development: Lessons and Experiences From Abroad', South African Mining Development Association.

CHAPTER 6: ASIA

INTRODUCTION

According to the National Bureau of Asian Research (NBR), 'energy and resource security have become critical strategic issues in Asia as energy demand and import dependence rise rapidly. Regional powers have responded with nationalist and mercantilist strategies to secure control over energy and commodity supplies'.[286] As a result, national oil companies (NOCs) are increasingly engaged in a scramble for security of gas and oil supply. In contrast to the past thirty years, where support for NOCs was dwindling, in recent times Asian states are increasing their support for NOCs. We are beginning to see mercantilist approaches in relation to the energy sector.

The resource nationalism of most of the Asian countries follows a hybrid model: a mixture of foreign direct investment and domestic commercial and trade strategies. This is largely because many of the Asian countries are net-importers of natural resources and their major concern, therefore, is energy and resource security. Domestic production alone is not sufficient to meet growing energy needs.

None of the Asian countries are major oil exporters. In fact, they are, to varying degrees, oil dependent. Given the scale of the needs of the Chinese economy, the country has a significant influence on global commodity prices, so its approach to energy is mainly driven by energy and resource security considerations. China and India are expected to account for nearly half of the entire increase in global energy demand in the next 25 years, and this would shift the balance of global energy power.[287]

It is worth highlighting that resource nationalism in Asia does not seem tied to any particular ideological framework, nor does it appear to be a coherently framed strategy. Rather, it is a pragmatic approach to generate fiscal revenues, respond to socio-economic pressures, and achieve economic stability. There are cases such as China's rare earth protectionism (a stand-off with Japan over this resource) where there is apparent geopolitical use of resource nationalism.

---

286 NBR Report Brief. 2011. 'Asia's rising energy and resource nationalism – Implications for the United States, China and the Asian Pacific Region'.
287 Klare, M. T. 2008. *Rising Powers, Shrinking Planet: The New Geopolitics of Energy*, p. 64. New York: Henry Holt.

In some instances, it is a long-term strategy for energy security. But this is certainly not the overriding strategy for resource nationalism.

In the case of Indonesia, resource nationalism has been implemented on the back of high commodity prices, but also emerged as a move that coincided with the looming elections in the face of the waning popularity of President Susilo Bambang Yudhoyono, an election which he did not contest.

This chapter discusses the resurgence of resource nationalism in Asia, with specific reference to three major players: Indonesia, India and China.

INDONESIA

The energy sector

In 2013, Indonesia ranked as the 24th largest producer of crude oil, according to British Petroleum's Statistical Review of World Energy 2013, with one per cent of the world's production. International oil companies in the Indonesian oil market include Chevron, Total, ConocoPhillips, ExxonMobil and British Petroleum (BP). Chevron is the largest oil producer in Indonesia, accounting for about 39 per cent of the country's crude production in 2013. PT Pertamina, Indonesia's state-owned integrated energy supply company, accounted for approximately 17 per cent of domestic crude production through 2012, according to government reports.[288]

Indonesia possessed 3.6 billion barrels of proven crude oil reserves as of January 2014, down from four billion barrels at the beginning of 2013, according to *Oil & Gas Journal* (OGJ).

The *Oil & Gas Journal* further reports that Indonesia possessed 104.4 trillion cubic feet of proven natural gas reserves in 2014, down from 108.4 trillion cubic feet in 2013. The country ranks as the 13th largest holder of proven natural gas reserves in the world, and the second largest in the Asia-Pacific region after China. Its gas sector is dominated by IOCs. The United States Energy Information Administration (EIA) estimates that Indonesia produced 2.6 trillion cubic feet of gas in 2012, mostly from offshore fields.

Indonesia remains the world's largest exporter of coal by weight, and exports about 75 per cent of its production, according to the EIA. Coal is predominantly used for power generation domestically. According to EIA figures, Indonesia's coal consumption grew to 76 million short tonnes in 2012.

---

288 Klare, M. T. 2008. *Rising Powers, Shrinking Planet: The New Geopolitics of Energy*, p. 64. New York: Henry Holt.

Sector regulation

Mining in Indonesia is an important economic activity. It contributes between five and six per cent of the gross domestic product (GDP). In 2010, Indonesia imposed a 'domestic market obligation on large coal producers, requiring that about 24 per cent of all supply be sold in the domestic market'.[289] In 2012, as part of a move towards further resource nationalism, 'the country adopted an export ban for unprocessed raw ores and stones, taking everyone by surprise'.[290]

In terms of new regulations (the Implementation of Mineral and Coal Mining Business Activities) adopted in 2012, 'foreign investment companies with mineral and coal mining licences and special mining business licences are required to divest a minimum of 51 per cent of their shares to Indonesian companies. The divestment must be executed in the fifth to tenth year after they start production'.[291] Expectedly, the new regulation has caused ructions in the mining industry, with many players alleging that it amounts to nationalisation.

There are varied explanations for this move, but it is seen as an example of resource nationalism in Indonesia. It has been invariably attributed to an increase in government's confidence as demand for Indonesia's resources have risen, and foreign direct investment surged to US$5.92 billion for the first quarter in 2012, 16 per cent of which is made up of mining.

In 2014, Indonesia imposed a ban on the export of raw materials. The Indonesian government forced mining companies to process minerals at home so as to preserve and domesticate profits. This can also be interpreted to mean that there is a drive to beneficiate locally with the aim of improving growth, competitiveness and job creation.

CHINA

According to Chatham House, countries such as China and India are dominating the global market for metals and coal, both as producers and consumers, with the latter dimension becoming more pronounced[292]. Import dependence will be more so for hydrocarbons. Despite featuring in the global top 10 of oil producers, China is forced to depend on other countries in the Gulf and Africa to meet its energy needs. This is the case, too, for India, which competes with China, along with other established powers, in *resources commercial activism* in Africa and elsewhere.

---

289 Ibid.

290 Klaassens, W. 2012. 'Resource Nationalism Threatens Indonesia', *Global Trade Review*, p. 54–56.

291 *Indonesia Finance Today*, 7 March 2012. Available at: http://www.geckoresearch.com/Indonesia-Foreign_Mining_Companies_Required_to_Divest_51pct_of_Shares [Accessed 5 May 2014].

292 Lee, B., et al. 2012. 'Resources Future: A Chatham House Report'. Available at: http://www.chathamhouse.org/sites/default/files/public/Research/Energy,%20Environment%20and%20Development/1212r_resourcesfutures.pdf [Accessed: 26 April 2014].

Energy sector

According to the US Energy Information Administration (EIA), 'China is the world's second largest oil consumer behind the US and became the largest global energy consumer in 2010'.[293] This is due to its rapid industrialisation and population size.

According to the OGJ, as of January 2014, 'China holds 24.4 billion barrels of proven oil reserves ... the highest in the Asia-Pacific region'.[294] In 2009, China became the second largest oil importer after the US.

The World Energy Council estimates that China had 'an estimated 126 billion short tonnes of recoverable coal reserves in 2011, the third largest in the world behind the US and Russia'.[295] Today, coal comprises 69 per cent of total energy consumption in China.

According to OGJ estimates, 'China held 155 trillion cubic feet of proven natural gas reserves as of January 2014 ... the largest in the Asia Pacific region.' CNPC accounts for about 73 per cent of production. China's natural gas pricing is regulated and is 'generally below international market rates'.

Sovereign Wealth Funds

Sovereign wealth funds are simply state-owned investment funds capitalised from balance of payments surpluses, foreign currency operations, proceeds from privatisation, fiscal surpluses and proceeds from commodity exports.[296] Their objectives are as varied as their expressions.

China's major sovereign wealth fund was created in 2007 in accordance with China's Company Law and capitalised with US$200 billion from the Chinese central bank's massive pile of foreign exchange reserves.[297] Its ongoing capitalisation is through Treasury bond issuance.

Sector regulation

Over the past 15 years, Chinese NOCs have been growing in significance. China has three key national oil companies and they are both active abroad to secure long-term access to natural resources. The first of these is China Petroleum and Chemical Corporation (Sinopec), which is the largest and has a revenue base of US$428 billion. It is the fourth largest company in the world as measured by profits, according to Fortune 500. It is followed by another

293 US Energy Information Administration. 2014. 'Country Brief China'. Available at: (http://www.eia.gov/countries/country-data. cfm?fips=CH&trk=m) [Accessed 5 May 2014]

294 *Oil & Gas Journal*, quoted in EIA: (http://www.eia.gov/countries/cab.cfm?fips=CH) [Accessed 5 May 2014].

295 Ibid.

296 Curzio, A. Q. and Valeria Miceli. 2010. *Sovereign Wealth Funds: A Complete Guide to State-Owned Investment Funds*, pp. 19–20. London: Harriman House.

297 Bremmer, I. 2010. *The End of the Free Market: Who Wins the War Between States and Corporations?* New York: Penguin.

Resurgent Resource Nationalism? A Study Into The Global Phenomenon | Asia

107

Chinese state-owned oil company, the China National Petroleum Corporation (CNPC), with revenues of some US$408.6 billion. A third company, the China National Offshore Oil Corporation (CNOOC), focuses on offshore oil exploration and production.

In line with their outward-looking resource nationalism strategy, in the past year alone CNPC has invested nearly US$10 billion in oil and gas fields in Mozambique and Kazakhstan. Sinopec bought a 33 per cent stake in another Fortune 500 company, Apache Egypt's fields, for US$3.1 billion. In 2012 CNOOC bought into Canada's Nexen with an eye on oil sands and shale gas production.[298]

Chinese leaders see strong diplomatic ties and joint ventures between Chinese national energy companies and foreign entities as a key strategy to ensure security of supply. Various Chinese national oil companies have structured alliances or joint ventures with state-owned oil firms of countries such as Angola (Sonangol), Nigeria (Nigerian National Petroleum Corporation), Russia (Gazprom) and Venezuela's PDVSA.[299] These alliances are forged either to develop vast oil reserves, building energy infrastructure and logistics platforms, or developing refinery capacities.

'The Chinese government launched a fuel tax and reform of the domestic product pricing mechanism in 2009 in efforts to tie retail oil product prices more closely to international crude oil markets'.[300]

China's resource nationalism is centred on key priorities that the country's leaders have set: to diversify sources of imported energy; to rely on suppliers with overland connections with China, as opposed to maritime; and to entrust the procurement of foreign energy supplies to state-owned companies. Beyond constructing an oil pipeline in Kazakhstan, China has structured supply agreements with countries such as Algeria, Chad, Equatorial Guinea, Libya, Nigeria and Venezuela.

China's rare earth

China has the largest rare earth reserves in the world, accounting for about 46.4 per cent of global share, and it accounts for 98 per cent of the world output.[301] Rare earth elements are important resources for clean-energy technology and high manufacturing. More importantly, this resource is strategic for China's energy technological revolution.

298   *CNN Money.* 2013. 'China is on Oil and Gas Shopping Spree', 30 October. Available at: http://money.cnn.com/2013/10/30/news/economy/china-energy-mergers/index.html [Accessed: 21 April 2014].

299   Klare, M. T. 2010. *Rising Powers, Shrinking Planet: The New Geopolitics of Energy*, p. 76. New York: Henry Holt.

300   Ibid.

301   Hao, Y. and Weihua, Liu. 2011. 'Rare Earth Minerals and Commodity Resource Nationalism', *The National Bureau of Asian Research, NBR Special Report 31*, p. 41.

The example of resource nationalism over this particular commodity was evident when China's Ministry of Commerce announced in 2010 that it would cut rare earth element exports by 72 per cent. The US immediately brought the case before the World Trade Organisation (WTO) Dispute Settlement Mechanism for adjudication. China has, at one point, used its dominance of this strategic commodity to starve Japan of exports in retaliation for the detention of a Chinese fishing boat captain after ship collisions near the disputed Senkanku Islands in the East China Sea, prompting fears that China may in future use its dominance of rare earths for geopolitical reasons. These tensions, generated by resource nationalism, remain. The official view of the Chinese government is that curtailing rare earth production has nothing to do with geopolitics, but more about limiting damage to the environment caused by illegal mining and smuggling. Nakano points out that there are legitimate environmental concerns in China that cannot be ignored.[302]

INDIA

India also follows the hybrid model of resource nationalism as explained above. The high energy demand makes the country heavily dependent on imported crude oil. The gap between demand and supply is widening whilst domestic production remains largely flat. Generally, India is a net oil importer. In the 1970s and 80s, India followed a policy of nationalisation. In 1991, the country started opening up and encouraged 'market competition', in other words, privatisation and liberalisation of the energy sector. Even though the energy sector market is open, investment is still relatively low.

Energy sector
India was the fourth largest consumer of oil and petroleum products after the US, China, and Japan in 2013. The country's net oil imports stand at 71 per cent in 2012, up from 42 per cent in 1990. 'Despite being a net importer of crude oil, India has become a net exporter of petroleum products by investing in refineries designed for export, particularly in Gujarat'.[303]

According to OGJ, 'India held nearly 5.7 billion barrels of proved oil reserves at the beginning of 2014. About 44 per cent are onshore resources, while 56 per cent are offshore'.[304] Even though this is the case, India's production capacity is still very low, hence the country's heavy oil import dependence. In fact, the marginal production taking place is also on the decline, despite plans to

302 Nakano, J. 2011. 'Rare Earth Trade Challenges and Sino-Japanese Relations: A Rise of Resource Nationalism' in *The National Bureau of Asian Research, NBR Special Report 31*, p. 41.

303 http://www.eia.gov/countries/cab.cfm?fips=IN? [Accessed 5 May 2014].

304 Ibid.

Resurgent Resource Nationalism? A Study Into The Global Phenomenon | *Asia*

109

increase production by 2030. The government encourages foreign acquisition of oil through Foreign Direct Investment (FDI) and various partnerships forged by India's NOCs.

In the coal stakes, India is the third largest consumer in the world. The state has a near monopoly over the coal sector. 'India's government took control of the country's coal reserves with the 1973 Coal Mines Nationalisation Act, establishing Coal India Limited (CIL) in 1975 as the state-owned sole producer and aggregating coal production and investment. In 2007, the government passed the New Coal Distribution Policy that attempted to allocate limited coal supplies to priority sectors, particularly the power and fertiliser industries, and India's 12th Five-Year Plan calls for CIL to link indigenous coal production with part of the fuel requirements of power plant projects coming online by 2017'.[305]

The OGJ documents that India had 47 trillion cubic feet of proven natural gas reserves at the beginning of 2014. The EIA reports that 'the country was self-sufficient in natural gas until 2004, when it began to import liquefied natural gas (LNG) from Qatar ... the Ministry of Petroleum and Natural Gas' (MOPNG) Directorate of Hydrocarbons functions as an upstream regulator and monitors coal bed methane projects. Until 2006, the Gas Authority of India Limited (GAIL) functioned as a near monopoly operating India's natural gas pipelines'.[306]

According to OGJ, total gas production in India amounted to around 1.5 trillion cubic feet in 2012. The two biggest state-owned companies, ONGC and Oil India Ltd (OIL), dominate India's upstream gas sector'.[307]

National Oil Companies

Since 1999, the government has been issuing licences for 100 per cent ownership by IOCs. The New Exploration Licensing Policy (NELP) allows 'investors to bid on development blocks up to 100 per cent foreign control ... competition in the oil sector is now relatively open, particularly when it comes to the upstream market'. The Ministry of Petroleum and Natural Gas (MOPNG) 'regulates the entire value chain of the oil sector'.[308]

India also has NOCs that are active abroad to find sources of vital resources to meet the economy's growing demand for raw material inputs. India's state-

305 Ibid.
306 Ibid.
307 *Oil & Gas Journal*, quoted in US Energy Information Administration: http://www.eia.gov/countries/cab.cfm?fips=IN [Accessed 5 May 2014].
308 *Oil & Gas Journal*, quoted in US Energy Information Administration: http://www.eia.gov/countries/cab.cfm?fips=IN [Accessed 5 May 2014].

owned energy firms are Oil and Natural Gas Corporation (ONGC), Indian Oil Corporation (Indian Oil) and the Hindustan Petroleum Corporation. Through state-owned enterprises, public policy and market regulation, 'energy security takes a central position in government policymaking'.[309]

Effectively, the Indian government also follows the strategy of local and international partnerships. The IOCs are an important part of the energy strategy and architecture.

Unconventional tools: Export taxes

Apart from the more conventional tools of promoting resource nationalism such as formation of sovereign wealth funds, taxation, equity, etc., countries also deploy restrictive measures intended to protect competitiveness up the value chain in resources sectors by limiting the export of key inputs that are considered strategic. These include export restrictions and export taxes. An export restriction is defined by the WTO as a 'border measure that takes the form of a government law or regulation, which expressly limits the quantity of exports, or places explicit conditions on the circumstances under which exports are permitted or that takes the form of a government imposed fee or tax on exports of the product calculated to limit the quantity of exports'.

Asian countries have been some of the most active in the use of export restrictive measures on their natural resources and agriculture. There are different types of export restrictions: (1) an outright ban on exports; (2) quantitative export restrictions; (3) quotas; (4) automatic and non-automatic licensing and export taxes. Quantitative restrictions assume the form of limits in quantities of commodities that are allowed to be exported. Export licence requirements establish that 'an application or other documents should be submitted as a condition for exportation and, depending on whether licence acquisition is automatic, the application may affect the volume of exports'.[310]

Despite its restrictive nature on the use of 'export restrictions' of a non-tariff form, the General Agreement on Trade and Tariffs (GATT) does not prohibit export taxes or production limits. Since export taxes take the form of a tariff duty, they are thus permitted under the WTO. In the period between 2009 and 2011, the following Asian countries have used export restrictions or duties on mineral products (WTO, 2011).[311]

*   India (iron ore products and scrap material)

309 International Energy Agency. 2012. 'Understanding Energy Challenges in India: Policies, Players and Issues'. Available at: https://www.iea.org/publications/freepublications/publication/India_study_FINAL_WEB.pdf [Accessed: 25 April 2014].

310 Ibid.

311 World Trade Organisation. (2011). Report on G20 Trade Measures: Mid-October 2010 to April 2011. www.wto.org/english/news_e/news11.../g20_wto_report_may11_e.doc [Accessed 5 May 2014].

* China (rare earth elements)
* Vietnam (sand, stones, and mineral products)
* Indonesia (mining products).

China, in particular, has been applying export restrictions and production limits on its rare-earth minerals and a range of other minerals, with very little challenge from other countries, with the exception of the US in the WTO. This has sparked off geopolitical tensions with Japan, which view these rare earth inputs as important for the production of certain technologies. China has recently lost the case brought against it by the US at the hands of the WTO Dispute Settlement Mechanism.

There are various reasons why countries resort to export taxes. For least developed countries this is mostly for revenue generation purposes. Many developing or middle-income countries, for example India and Indonesia, would not ordinarily resort to export taxes to shore up their fiscal revenues since they tend to have more diversified economies and therefore revenue sources. A number of countries use these measures to promote downstream sectors in the mining or manufacturing value chain.

Restricting the exportation of certain raw materials helps to secure their availability for scaling-up the value-chain, while limiting the competitiveness of competitor countries on high-tech products. Resource security is never for its own sake, but often motivated by either developmental objectives or strategic goals such as facilitating structural diversification of the economy and production processes. As highlighted in the case of Indonesia, this is also inspired by politics, especially to capture the loyalty of indigenous capital.

CONCLUSION

The three cases discussed in this chapter illustrate the fact that Asia has also been affected by resurgent resource nationalism. For India and China, rising energy demands have resulted in the countries becoming net importers of energy resources. This trend is likely to continue for the next decade or two due to population size and industrialisation.

In Asia, unconventional methods are combined with conventional ones to bring about a hybrid model to achieve resource nationalism. This hybrid model, as stated above, aims to project a resource nationalism that is inward- and outward-looking simultaneously. India and China, for instance, as net importers, are rapidly making use of NOCs to acquire energy resources across the world.

Like most jurisdictions in the world, the new face of resource nationalism takes the form of partnerships between the private and the public sectors. Therefore, opportunities for partnerships between NOCs and IOCs abound. Whereas India aggressively encourages such partnerships, Indonesia requires that foreign investors cede 51 per cent of their company shares to local Indonesian companies. China has a heavy presence of active NOCs domestically, combined with FDI strategies abroad.

In countries like China, unique opportunities to invest and partner with NOCs are further highlighted in the massive rare earth elements endowment. This is crucial because rare earth elements are important for the manufacturing of cleaner energy technologies. A partnership in this area can yield win-win results for both IOCs and NOCs.

CHAPTER 7: CONCLUSION

In broad terms, this report deals with the involvement of the states of richly endowed nations in their natural resources. To be sure, state involvement in the economy is not a new phenomenon in political society. History is replete with instances of state involvement in the economy – from as far back as the sixteenth century, from mercantilism to contemporary socialist economies, continuing up to the recent period following the 2008 global financial crisis.

Across time and space, state involvement in the economy has taken different forms and produced different outcomes. Even neoliberal economics, defined loosely as 'withdrawal of the state', is itself a form of state involvement. The state is never absent in the political economy. It is the nature of the involvement that changes. Throughout the report, it is important to observe that resource nationalism is not confined to authoritarian or socialist-leaning governments as the dominant myth suggests; in fact, it cuts across the political spectrum.

After a systematic study of various primary and secondary sources of literature, this study affirms the commonly held view that the world is experiencing a resurgence of resource nationalism. Due to their strategic value, energy resources are the most affected by this resurgence.

KEY FINDINGS

At a high level, some of the key findings are summarised as follows:

* The 2001–2008 'commodities boom' saw oil prices soaring with private players in the energy sector making super-profits. Consequently, resurgent 'resource nationalism' was encountered in many resource-rich countries throughout the world.
* The phenomenon of resource nationalism takes on different forms and varying pace in countries and regions across the globe. More importantly, recent forms of resource nationalism have used diverse instruments compared to the outright state nationalisation of previous decades.
* As can be seen in the various chapters, key drivers of resource nationalism are common to almost all the selected countries, and they are: ideology and politics, local community demands, socio-economic elements (including the 'commodities boom'), as well as the fluid contractual and legislative environment.

- High among the key drivers are: 'local community demands' and the recent 'commodities boom'. This means that the convergence of domestic and global pressures and opportunities produces a climate of heavier state involvement in the natural resources sector.
- Drivers like 'local community demands' are unlikely to change over time. The expectation of the people that they should benefit from their natural resources is something that is deeply embedded in communities as a matter of social justice.

* In simple terms, resource nationalism refers to increasing financial, regulatory and operational control in the natural resources sector by state actors.

* In the report, two major forms of resource nationalism are identifiable: first is the form that can be defined as 'inward-looking' and, second, the unusual 'outward-looking' form. The distinction is primarily based on the origins and location of the natural resources:

- By 'inward-looking' resource nationalism one refers to the kind that is realised through utilising abundant natural resources beneath the soil within a sovereign state's territory. The African and Latin American regions are the best examples of this form.
- On the other hand, 'outward-looking' resource nationalism is realised when a net importer, usually with little natural endowments or production in its territory, deploys various instruments such as sovereign wealth funds, export restrictions, as well as foreign direct investment initiatives, to acquire natural resources abroad. The Asian region is the best example in this regard.

* The report is specifically biased towards hydrocarbons (oil, coal and gas) due to their strategic value as energy sources. For many governments, a pragmatic approach has been adopted: if international oil companies (IOCs) reap super profits during boom years, governments must maximise benefits for the 'people' by demanding higher resource rents. For their part, IOCs adapt to changing policy environments by conceding to government demands whilst making reasonable profits. As shown in the study, these companies (IOCs) engage in various ventures with national oil companies (NOCs) to survive the recent wave of resource nationalism. The dominant tendency is engagement rather than withdrawal. It appears that major energy players are seeking 'win-win' situations in their engagement with resource nationalism.

* For countries like China, with rare earth as an abundant natural resource, the strategy is to diversify their participation in the energy value chain. Rare earth elements are important for new clean energy technologies. Therefore, beyond increasing resource rents, China looks forward to dominating the domestic and global markets in downstream activities.

* As in earlier decades, the role of IOCs, even though drastically curtailed and even threatened in some jurisdictions, remains critical to better human and economic outcomes in the future. Many IOCs are taking advantage of the new

emerging partnerships with state actors and are already making the most of the changing policy environment.

* International oil companies, such as Sasol and BP, have greater leverage in forging partnerships with NOCs in jurisdictions of their interest simply because of their long-standing reputation as leaders in energy technology and technical 'know how'. Such IOCs are better positioned to ride the current wave of resource nationalism.

WHAT REMAINS AS CERTAINTY IN THE NATURAL RESOURCES SECTOR TODAY?

Simply put, the one certainty that remains is the sovereign right of states, guaranteed under international law, that all natural resources beneath the soil fall under their territorial jurisdiction. Everything else is subject to change. The only way to violate this sovereign right is by war or some other form of aggression or takeover. As it stands, there is only one route to gain access to natural resource rights, which is through various forms of state licences to extract, process, and trade.

Finally, it is apparent that, for politico-economic reasons, all countries are engaged in the scramble for either fossil fuels or new sources of energy and new related technologies. The overriding concern of states is to ensure security of supply, and that alone makes energy a strategic concern and one which shapes decisions on investment and geopolitics.

APPENDIX
Table 1
Europe: Selected Indicators for 2012 (Countries Ranked by GDP)

	Country	Population	Area	GDP Per Capita	GDP	% of Total	Cumulative % of Total
1.	Germany	81 726 000	357 022	41 514	3 428.1	17.0	17.0
2.	France	65 437 000	551 500	39 772	2 612.9	12.9	29.9
3.	UK	62 641 000	243 610	38 514	2 475.9	12.3	42.2
4.	Russia	141 930 000	17 098 242	14 037	2 014.8	10.0	52.2
5.	Italy	60 770 000	301 340	33 049	2 014.7	10.0	62.2
6.	Spain	46 235 000	505 370	29 195	1 323.0	6.6	68.8
7.	Netherlands	16 696 000	41 543	46 054	777.6	3.9	72.7
8.	Switzerland	7 907 000	41 277	79 052	631.2	3.1	75.8
9.	Sweden	9 453 000	450 295	55 245	523.9	2.6	78.4
10.	Norway	4 952 000	323 802	99 558	500.0	2.5	80.9
11.	Poland	38 216 000	312 685	12 708	489.8	2.4	83.3
12.	Belgium	11 008 000	30 528	43 413	483.3	2.4	85.7
13.	Austria	8 419 000	83 871	47 226	394.7	2.0	87.7
14.	Denmark	5 631 000	2 209 180	56 210	315.2	1.6	89.3
15.	Greece	11 304 000	131 957	22 083	249.1	1.2	90.5
16.	Finland	5 387 000	338 145	46 179	247.5	1.2	91.7
17.	Portugal	10 637 000	92 090	20 182	212.3	1.1	92.8
18.	Ireland	4 487 000	70 283	45 836	210.8	1.0	93.8
19.	Czech Republic	10 546 000	78 867	18 608	196.4	1.0	94.8
20.	Ukraine	45 706 000	603 550	3 867	176.3	0.9	95.7
21.	Romania	21 390 000	238 391	7 943	169.4	0.8	96.5
22.	Hungary	9 971 000	93 028	12 622	124.6	0.6	97.1
23.	Slovakia	5 440 000	49 035	16 934	91.1	0.5	97.6
24.	Belarus	9 473 000	207 600	6 685	63.3	0.3	97.9
25.	Croatia	4 407 000	56 594	13 227	59.2	0.3	98.2
26.	Luxembourg	517 000	2 586	107 476	55.2	0.3	98.5
27.	Bulgaria	7 476 000	110 879	6 986	51.0	0.3	98.8
28.	Slovenia	2 052 000	20 273	22 092	45.3	0.2	99.0
29.	Lithuania	3 203 000	65 300	14 150	42.3	0.2	99.2
30.	Serbia	7 261 000	77 474	5 190	37.5	0.2	99.4
31.	Latvia	2 220 000	64 589	14 009	28.4	0.1	99.5
32.	Cyprus	1 117 000	9 251	26 315	22.8	0.1	99.6
33.	Estonia	1 340 000	45 228	16 316	22.4	0.1	99.7
34.	Bosnia	3 752 000	51 197	4 487	17.5	0.1	99.8
35.	Iceland	319 000	103 000	42 658	13.6	0.1	99.9
36.	Albania	3 216 000	28 748	4 000	12.6	0.1	100.0

Resurgent Resource Nationalism? A Study Into The Global Phenomenon | Appendix

117

37.	Macedonia	2 064 000	25 713	4 589	9.6	0.0
38.	Malta	419 000	316	20 848	8.7	0.0
39.	Moldova	3 559 000	33 851	2 038	7.3	0.0
40.	Monaco	37 579	2	163 026	6.4	0.0
41.	Lichtenstein	36 657	160	134 617	6.2	0.0
42.	Montenegro	632 000	13 812	6 813	4.4	0.0
43.	Andorra	78 360	468	46 418	3.6	0.0
44.	San Marino	31 247	61	62 188	2.0	0.0
45.	Vatican City	-	-	-	-	
	TOTAL	**739 100 000**	**25 162 713**		**20 190.6**	

Sources: World Development Indicators Database; UNData

Website: United States Geological Service (USGS)

Table 2

European Countries: Country Groups and Categories

	European Countries	Advanced Countries (IMF)	European Union	Eurozone
1.	Austria	Yes	Yes	Yes
2.	Albania	No	No	No
3.	Andorra	No	No	No
4.	Belarus	No	No	No
5.	Belgium	No	Yes	Yes
6.	Bosnia	No	No	No
7.	Bulgaria	No	Yes	No
8.	Croatia	No	Yes	No
9.	Cyprus	Yes	Yes	Yes
10.	Czech Republic	Yes	Yes	No
11.	Denmark	Yes	Yes	No
12.	Estonia	Yes	Yes	Yes
13.	Finland	Yes	Yes	Yes
14.	France	Yes	Yes	Yes
15.	Germany	Yes	Yes	Yes
16.	Greece	Yes	Yes	Yes
17.	Hungary	No	Yes	No
18.	Iceland	Yes	No	No
19.	Ireland	Yes	Yes	Yes
20.	Italy	Yes	Yes	Yes
21.	Latvia	Yes	Yes	Yes
22.	Liechtenstein	No	No	No
23.	Lithuania	No	Yes	No
24.	Luxembourg	Yes	Yes	Yes
25.	Macedonia	No	No	No
26.	Malta	Yes	Yes	Yes
27.	Moldova	No	No	No
28.	Monaco	No	No	No
29.	Montenegro	No	No	No
30.	Netherlands	Yes	Yes	Yes
31.	Norway	Yes	No	No
32.	Poland	No	Yes	No
33.	Portugal	Yes	Yes	No
34.	Romania	No	Yes	No
35.	Russia	No	No	No
36.	San Marino	Yes	No	No

37.	Serbia	No	No	No
38.	Slovakia	Yes	Yes	Yes
39.	Slovenia	Yes	Yes	Yes
40.	Spain	Yes	Yes	Yes
41.	Sweden	Yes	Yes	No
42.	Switzerland	Yes	No	No
43.	Ukraine	No	No	No
44.	United Kingdom	Yes	Yes	No
	Number of Countries	26	28	18

Source: IMF Data and Statistics Website

Table 3
European Union Population and GDP (2012)

	European Union Countries	Population	GDP
1.	Austria	8 419 000	394.7
2.	Belgium	11 008 000	483.3
3.	Bulgaria	7 476 000	51.0
4.	Croatia	4 407 000	59.2
5.	Cyprus	1 117 000	22.8
6.	Czech Republic	10 546 000	196.4
7.	Denmark	5 631 000	315.2
8.	Estonia	1 340 000	22.4
9.	Finland	5 387 000	247.5
10.	France	65 437 000	2 612.9
11.	Germany	81 726 000	3 428.1
12.	Greece	11 304 000	249.1
13.	Hungary	9 971 000	124.6
14.	Ireland	4 487 000	210.8
15.	Italy	60 770 000	2 014.7
16.	Latvia	2 220 000	28.4
17.	Lithuania	3 203 000	42.3
18.	Luxembourg	517 000	55.2
19.	Malta	419 000	8.7
20.	Netherlands	16 696 000	777.6
21.	Poland	38 216 000	489.8
22.	Portugal	10 637 000	212.3
23.	Romania	21 390 000	169.4
24.	Slovakia	5 440 000	91.0
25.	Slovenia	2 052 000	45.3
26.	Spain	46 235 000	1 323.0
27.	Sweden	9 453 000	523.9
28.	United Kingdom	62 641 000	2 475.9
	Total	**508 145 000**	**16 675.5**

Sources: World Development Indicators Database; UNData Website

Table 4
Eurozone Population and GDP (2012)

	European Union Countries	Population	GDP
1.	Austria	8 419 000	394.7
2.	Belgium	11 008 000	483.3
3.	Cyprus	1 117 000	22.8
4.	Estonia	1 340 000	22.4
5.	Finland	5 387 000	247.5
6.	France	65 437 000	2 612.9
7.	Germany	81 726 000	3 428.1
8.	Greece	11 304 000	249.1
9.	Ireland	4 487 000	210.8
10.	Italy	60 770 000	2 014.7
11.	Latvia	2 220 000	28.4
12.	Luxembourg	517 000	55.2
13.	Malta	419 000	8.7
14.	Netherlands	16 696 000	777.6
15.	Portugal	10 637 000	212.3
16.	Romania	21 390 000	169.4
17.	Slovakia	5 440 000	91.0
18.	Slovenia	2 052 000	45.3
	Total	**310 366 000**	**11 074.2**

Sources: World Development Indicators Database; UNData Website

Table 5

Per Capita GDP Growth Rates: USSR & Russia, Norway, United Kingdom, Finland, Western Europe, Eastern Europe, and United States

Country/ Country Group	1820–1870 Initial phase of capitalist development	1870–1913 Old liberal order	1913–1950 Inter–war years	1950–1973 Golden era	1973–2008 Neoliberal order
USSR	0.63	1.06	1.76	3.35	0.76
Norway	0.52	1.3	2.13	3.19	2.67
United Kingdom	1.26	1.01	0.93	2.42	1.96
Finland	0.76	1.44	1.91	4.25	2.27
Western Europe	0.98	1.33	0.76	4.05	1.93
Eastern Europe	0.63	1.39	0.60	3.81	1.55
United States	1.34	1.82	1.61	2.45	1.80

Source: Maddison (2006) and Maddison (2010)

Table 6

Per Capita GDP Levels: USSR and Russia, Norway, United Kingdom, Finland, Western Europe, Eastern Europe and United States

Country/ Country Group	1820	1870	1913	1950	1973	2008
USSR	688	943	1488	2841	6 059	7 904
Norway	1 104	1 432	2 501	5 463	11 246	24 344
United Kingdom	1 706	3 190	4 921	6 939	12 025	23 742
Finland	781	1 140	2 111	4 253	11 085	24 344
Western Europe	1 204	1960	3 458	4 579	11 416	22 246
United States	1 257	2 445	5 301	9 561	16 689	8 569
Africa	420	500	637	894	1 410	1 780

Source: Maddison (2006) and Maddison (2010)

Table 7

European Production of Mineral Fuels

	European production	Percentage of world production	Russia as a percentage of European production	European (excl. Russia) percentage of world production
Oil	13.4mbpd	16.1	76.3	3.8
Natural Gas	869bn³	25.8	68.1	8.2
Coal	1 035mt	13.2	32.3	8.9
Uranium	4 153tu	7.1	69.1	2.2

Table 8

World Oil Reserves in 2012 (Top Countries)

		Oil Reserves (billion barrels)	% of Total	Cumulative % of Total
1.	Venezuela	297.6	17.8	17.8
2.	Saudi Arabia	265.9	15.9	33.7
3.	Canada	173.9	10.4	44.1
4.	Iran	157.0	9.4	53.5
5.	Iraq	150.0	9.0	62.5
6.	Kuwait	101.5	6.1	68.6
7.	UAE	97.0	5.9	74.5
8.	Russia	87.2	5.2	79.7
9.	Libya	48.0	2.9	82.6
10.	Nigeria	37.2	2.2	84.8
11.	US	35.0	2.1	86.9
12.	Kazakhstan	30.0	1.8	88.7
	TOTAL	**1668.9**		

Table 9
World Oil Production in 2012 (Top Countries)

		Oil Production (thousand barrels/ day)	% of Total	Cumulative % of Total
1.	Saudi Arabia	11 530	13.3	13.3
2.	Russia	10 643	12.8	26.1
3.	United States	8 905	9.6	35.7
4.	China	4 074	5.0	40.7
5.	Canada	3 741	4.4	45.1
6.	Iran	3 680	4.2	49.3
7.	UAE	3 380	3.7	53.0
8.	Kuwait	3 127	3.7	56.7
9.	Iraq	3 115	3.7	60.4
10.	Mexico	2 911	3.5	63.9
11.	Venezuela	2 725	3.4	67.3
12.	Nigeria	2 417	2.8	70.1
13.	Brazil	2 149	2.7	72.8
14.	Norway	1 916	2.1	74.9
	TOTAL	**86 152**		

Table 10
European Oil Production in 2012 (Top Countries)

		Oil Production (thousand barrels/ day)	% of Total	Cumulative % of Total
1.	Russia	10 643	76.3	76.3
2.	Norway	1 916	13.8	90.1
3.	United Kingdom	967	6.9	97.0
4.	Denmark	207	1.5	98.5
5.	Italy	112	0.8	99.3
6.	Romania	86	0.6	99.9
	TOTAL	**13 391**		
		(16.1% of world production)		

Table 11
World Natural Gas Reserves in 2012 (Top Countries)

		Natural Gas Reserves (trillion cubic feet)	% of Total	Cumulative % of Total
1.	Iran	1 187.3	18.0	18.0
2.	Russia	1 162.5	17.6	35.6
3.	Qatar	885.1	13.4	49.0
4.	Turkmenistan	618.1	9.3	58.3
5.	United States	300.0	4.5	62.8
6.	UAE	215.1	3.3	66.1
7.	Venezuela	196.4	3.0	69.1
8.	Nigeria	182.0	2.8	71.9
9.	Algeria	159.1	2.4	74.3
10.	Australia	132.8	2.0	76.3
11.	China	109.3	1.7	78.0
	TOTAL	**6 614.1**		

Table 12.
World Natural Gas Reserves in 2012 (Top Countries)

		Natural Gas Reserves (billion cubic metres)	% of Total	Cumulative % of Total
1.	United States	681.4	20.4	20.4
2.	Russia	592.3	17.6	38.0
3.	Iran	160.5	4.8	42.8
4.	Qatar	157.0	4.7	47.5
5.	Canada	156.5	4.6	52.1
6.	Norway	114.9	3.4	55.5
7.	China	107.2	3.2	58.7
8.	Saudi Arabia	102.8	3.0	61.7
9.	Algeria	81.5	2.4	64.1
10.	Indonesia	71.1	2.1	66.2
	TOTAL	**3 363.9**		

Table 13
European Natural Gas Production in 2012 (Top Countries)

		Natural Gas (billion cubic metres)	% of Total	Cumulative % of Total
1.	Russia	592.3	68.1	68.1
2.	Norway	114.9	13.2	81.3
3.	Netherlands	63.9	7.4	88.7
4.	United Kingdom	41.0	4.7	93.4
5.	Ukraine	18.6	2.1	95.5
6.	Romania	10.9	1.3	96.8
7.	Germany	9.0	1.0	97.8
8.	Italy	7.8	0.9	98.7
9.	Denmark	6.4	0.7	99.4
10.	Poland	4.2	0.5	99.9
	TOTAL	**869.0**		
		(25.8% of world production)		

Table 14
World Coal Reserves in 2012 (Top Countries)

		Coal Reserves (million tonnes)	% of Total	Cumulative % of Total
1.	United States	237 295	27.6	27.6
2.	Russia	157 010	18.2	45.8
3.	China	114 500	13.3	59.1
4.	Australia	76 400	8.9	68.0
5.	India	60 600	7.0	75.0
6.	Germany	40 699	4.7	79.7
7.	Ukraine	33 833	3.9	83.6
8.	Kazakhstan	33 600	3.9	87.5
9.	South Africa	30 156	3.5	91.0
	TOTAL	**784 093**		

Source: BP Review of World Energy 2013

Table 15
World Coal Production in 2012 (Top Countries)

		Natural Gas (billion cuCoal production (million tonnes)	% of Total	Cumulative % of Total
1.	China	3 650.0	47.5	47.5
2.	United States	922.1	13.4	60.9
3.	India	605.8	6.0	66.9
4.	Australia	431.2	6.3	73.2
5.	Indonesia	386.0	6.2	79.4
6.	Russia	354.8	4.4	83.8
7.	South Africa	260.0	3.8	87.6
	TOTAL	7864.5		

Source: BP Review of World Energy Historical Data Workbook. The percentages of total are based on data expressed in tonnes oil equivalent

Table 16
European Coal Production in 2011 (Top Countries)

		Natural Gas (billion cuCoal production million tonnes)	% of Total	Cumulative % of Total
1.	Russia	334.8	32.3	32.3
2.	Germany	188.6	18.2	50.5
3.	Poland	139.3	13.5	64.0
4.	Ukraine	82.2	7.9	71.9
5.	Czech Republic	57.8	5.6	77.5
6.	Greece	54.0	5.2	82.7
7.	Others	178.7	17.3	100.0
	TOTAL	1035.4		
		(13.2% of world production)		

Source: United States Geological Service (USGS)

Table 17
World Uranium Production (2012)

		Uranium production (tonnes)	% of Total	Cumulative % of Total
1.	Kazakhstan	21 317	36.6	36.6
2.	Canada	8 999	15.4	52.0
3.	Australia	6 991	12.0	64.0
4.	Niger	4 667	8.0	72.0
5.	Namibia	4 495	7.7	79.7
6.	Uzbekistan	3 000	5.1	84.8
7.	Russia	2 872	4.9	89.7
8.	United States	1 596	2.7	92.4
9.	China	1 500	2.6	95.0
10.	Ukraine	960	1.6	96.6
11.	South Africa	465	0.8	97.4
12.	India	385	0.7	98.1
13.	Czech Republic	228	0.4	98.5
14.	Brazil	231	0.4	98.9
15.	Romania	90	0.2	99.1
16.	Germany	50	0.1	99.2
17.	Pakistan	45	0.1	99.3
18.	France	3	0.0	
	TOTAL	58 394		

Source: World Nuclear Association

Table 18

European Production of Uranium

		Uranium production (t onnes)	% of Total	Cumulative % of Total
1.	Russia	2 872	69.1	69.1
2.	Ukraine	960	23.1	92.2
3.	Czech Republic	228	5.5	97.7
4.	Romania	90	2.2	99.1
5.	France	3	0.1	100.0
TOTAL		**4 153**		
		(7.1% of world production)		

Source: World Nuclear Association

Table 19

World Production of Metallic Minerals in 2012

Minerals		Uranium Production Value ($billion)	% of Total	Cumulative % of Total
1.	Iron Ore	251.1	39	39
2.	Gold	103.0	16	54
3.	Copper	83.7	13	68
4.	Silver	19.3	3	71
5.	Nickel	19.3	3	74
6.	Potash	19.3	3	77
7.	Zinc	12.9	2	79
8.	PGMs	12.9	2	81
9.	Diamonds	12.9	2	83
10.	Phosphate Rock	12.9	2	85
11.	Others	96.6	15	100
	TOTAL	**644**		

Source: International Council on Metals and Mining (ICMM)

Table 20
World's Top Producers of Metallic Minerals in 2010

	Country	Production Value ($million)	% of Total Production Value	Cumulative % of Total Production Value
1.	Australia	71 955	15.6	15.6
2.	China	69 281	15.0	30.6
3.	Brazil	47 027	10.2	40.8
4.	Chile	31 275	6.8	47.6
5.	Russia	28 680	6.2	53.8
6.	South Africa	27 116	5.9	59.7
7.	India	26 042	5.6	65.3
8.	United States	22 957	5.0	70.3
9.	Peru	18 832	4.1	74.4
10.	Canada	13 984	3.0	77.4
11.	Indonesia	12 225	2.6	80.0
12.	Ukraine	9 283	2.0	82.0
	TOTAL	**463 759**		

Source: International Council on Metals and Mining (ICMM)

Table 21

European Production of Metallic Minerals in 2010

	Country	Production Value ($million)	Total Mineral Export Contribution	Production Value as % of GDP	% of Total Production Value	Cumulative % of Total
1.	Russia	28 680	6.6	1.9	59.3	59.3
2.	Ukraine	9 283	8.2	6.7	19.2	78.5
3.	Sweden	3 974	5.3	0.9	8.2	86.7
4.	Poland	3 051	4.7	0.7	6.3	93.0
5.	Bulgaria	699	17.5	1.5	1.4	94.4
6.	Finland	680	5.6	0.3	1.4	95.8
7.	Ireland	504	1.2	0.2	1.0	96.8
8.	Portugal	390	4.1	0.2	0.8	97.6
9.	Norway	333	6.4	0.1	0.7	98.3
10.	Greece	285	9.5	0.1	0.6	98.9
11.	Serbia	200	9.7	0.5	0.4	99.3
12.	Macedonia	190	0.0	2.1	0.4	99.7
13.	Germany	43	3.7	0.0	0.1	99.8
14.	Romania	19	4.2	0.0	0.0	
	TOTAL	**48 331**				
		(10.4% of world production)				

Source: International Council on Metals and Mining (ICMM). Mineral export contribution refers to mineral exports as a percentage of total exports

Table 22
European Production of Metallic Minerals in 2010

	European production	% of world production	Russian production	Russia as % of world production	Russia as % of European production	Europe (excl. Russia) % of world production
Aluminium	7.5mt	16.3	3.8mt	8.4	51.2	8.1
Antimony	6 500t	3.6	6 500t	3.6	100.0	0.0
Bauxite	9.3mt	3.6	5.9mt	2.3	63.5	1.3
Copper	1.4mt	9.0	713 000t	4.4	49.2	4.6
Gold	223 407kg	8.4	199 642kg	7.5	89.4	0.9
Iron Ore	211mt	7.2	100mt	3.4	47.4	3.8
Lead	348 000t	7.4	105 000t	2.2	30.2	5.2
Manganese	418 000t	2.5	30 000t	0.2	7.2	2.3
Mercury	50t	2.8	50t	2.8	100.0	0.0
Nickel	310 510t	16.0	267 000	13.8	86.0	2.2
Platinum	25 425kg	13.0	25 000kg	12.8	98.3	0.2
Silver	2 982kg	12.8	1350kg	5.8	45.3	7.0
Tin	190kg	0.1	160kg	0.1	84.2	0.0
Zinc	1mt	8.1	280 000t	2.2	27.0	5.9

Table 23
World Production of Primary Aluminium in 2012 (Top Producers)

	Country	Production (thousand tonnes)	% of Total Production	Cumulative % of Total Production
1.	China	20 300	44.2	44.2
2.	Russia	3 845	8.4	52.6
3.	Canada	2 781	6.1	58.7
4.	United States	2 070	4.5	63.2
5.	Australia	1 864	4.1	67.3
6.	UAE	1 820	4.0	71.3
7.	India	1 700	3.7	75.0
8.	Brazil	1 436	3.1	78.1
9.	Norway	1 145	2.5	80.6
	TOTAL	45 900		

Source: United States Geological Survey (USGS) 2012 Minerals Yearbook. The 2012 figures are estimates

Table 24

European Production of Primary Aluminium in 2012

	Country	% of European Production	% of Total Production	Cumulative % of Production
1.	Russia	3 845	51.2	51.2
2.	Norway	1 145	15.2	66.4
3.	Iceland	820	10.9	77.3
4.	Germany	410	5.5	82.8
5.	France	349	4.7	87.5
6.	Slovakia	161	2.1	89.6
7.	Netherlands	150	2.0	91.6
8.	Greece	135	1.8	93.4
9.	Sweden	129	1.7	95.1
10.	Bosnia	126	1.7	96.8
11.	Italy	110	1.5	98.3
12.	Montenegro	80	1.1	99.4
13.	Slovenia	40	0.5	99.9
	TOTAL	**7 500**		
		(16.3% of World)		

Source: United States Geological Survey (USGS) 2012 Minerals Yearbook. The 2012 figures are estimates

Table 25
World Production of Antimony in 2012

	Country	% of Production (Antimony content, tonnes)	% of Total Production	Cumulative % of Production
1.	China	150 000	83.5	83.5
2.	Canada	7 000	3.9	87.4
3.	Russia	6 500	3.6	91.0
4.	Bolivia	4 000	2.2	93.2
5.	South Africa	3 800	2.1	95.3
6.	Australia	2 481	1.4	96.7
7.	Tajikistan	2 000	1.1	97.8
8.	Turkey	1 900	1.1	98.9
	TOTAL	**179 681**		

Source: United States Geological Survey (USGS) 2012 Minerals Yearbook. The 2012 figures are estimates

Table 26
World Production of Bauxite in 2011

	Country	Production (thousand tonnes)	% of Total Production	Cumulative % of Production
1.	Australia	69 976	27.0	27.0
2.	China	45 000	17.4	44.4
3.	Indonesia	37 100	14.3	58.7
4.	Brazil	31 800	12.3	71.0
5.	India	19 000	7.3	78.3
6.	Guinea	17 593	6.8	85.1
7.	Jamaica	10 189	3.9	89.0
8.	Russia	5 890	2.3	91.3
9.	Venezuela	4 500	1.7	93.0
10.	Suriname	4 000	1.5	94.5
11.	Greece	2 100	0.8	95.3
12.	Guyana	1 818	0.7	96.0
13.	Sierra Leone	1 457	0.6	96.6
14.	Others	8 506	3.3	99.9
	TOTAL	**259 000**		

Source: United States Geological Survey (USGS) 2011 Minerals Yearbook. The 2011 figures are estimates.

Table 27
European Production of Bauxite in 2011

	Country	Production (thousand tonnes)	% of Total Production	Cumulative % of Production
1.	Russia	5 890	63.5	63.4
2.	Greece	2 100	22.6	86.0
3.	Bosnia	830	8.9	94.9
4.	Hungary	400	4.3	99.2
5.	Montenegro	60	0.6	99.8
	TOTAL	**9 280**		
	(3.6% of World Production)			

Source: United States Geological Survey (USGS) 2011 Minerals Yearbook. The 2011 figures are estimates

Table 28
World Mine Production of Copper in 2011

	Country	Production (thousand tonnes, copper content)	% of Total Production	Cumulative % of Production
1.	Chile	5 260	32.7	32.7
2.	China	1 310	8.1	40.8
3.	Peru	1 240	7.7	48.5
4.	United States	1 110	6.9	55.4
5	Australia	958	6.0	61.4
6.	Russia	713	4.4	65.8
7.	Zambia	668	4.1	69.9
8.	Canada	566	3.5	73.4
9.	Indonesia	543	3.4	76.8
10.	DRC	520	3.2	80.0
11.	Mexico	443	2.8	82.8
12.	Poland	427	2.7	85.5
13.	Kazakhstan	417	2.6	88.1
14.	Others	1 970	12.2	100.3
	TOTAL	**16 100**		

Source: United States Geological Survey (USGS) 2011 Minerals Yearbook. The 2011 figures are estimates

Table 29
World Production of Antimony in 2012

	Country	Production (tonnes, copper content)	% of Total Production	Cumulative % of Production
1.	Russia	713 000	49.2	49.2
2.	Poland	427 000	29.4	78.6
3.	Bulgaria	105 000	7.2	85.8
4.	Portugal	82 000	5.7	91.5
5.	Spain	68 400	4.7	96.2
6.	Serbia	29 300	2.0	98.2
7.	Finland	14 700	1.0	99.2
8.	Macedonia	7 900	0.5	99.7
9.	Romania	1 000	0.1	99.8
10.	Cyprus	200	0.0	
	TOTAL	**1 448 500**		
		(9.0% of World Production)		

Source: United States Geological Survey (USGS) 2011 Minerals Yearbook. The 2011 figures are estimates

Table 30
World Gold Production in 2011

	Country	Production (tonnes, gold content)	% of Total Production	Cumulative % of Production
1.	China	362	13.6	13.6
2.	Australia	258	9.7	23.3
3.	United States	234	8.8	32.1
4.	Russia	200	7.5	39.6
5.	South Africa	181	6.8	46.4
6.	Peru	164	6.1	52.5
7.	Canada	97	3.6	56.1
8.	Indonesia	96	3.6	59.7
9.	Uzbekistan	91	3.4	63.1
10.	Mexico	84	3.1	66.2
11.	Ghana	80	3.0	69.2
12.	Papua New Guinea	66	2.5	71.7
13.	Brazil	62	2.3	74.0
14.	Chile	45	1.7	75.7
15.	Others	640	24.1	99.8
	TOTAL	**2 660**		

Source: United States Geological Survey (USGS) 2011 Minerals Yearbook

Resurgent Resource Nationalism? A Study Into The Global Phenomenon | *Appendix*

139

Table 31
European Gold Production in 2011

	Country	Production (thousand tonnes)	% of Total Production	Cumulative % of Production
1.	Russia	199 642	89.4	89.4
2.	Finland	7 000	3.1	92.5
3.	Sweden	5 000	2.2	95.0
4.	Bulgaria	4 400	2.0	97.0
5.	Spain	3 500	1.6	98.6
6.	France	1 500	0.7	99.3
7.	Poland	500	0.2	99.5
8.	Italy	450	0.2	99.7
9.	Romania	400	0.2	99.9
10.	Serbia	360	0.2	100.1
11.	Slovakia	300	0.1	
12.	UK	202	0.1	
13.	Denmark	153	0.1	
	TOTAL	**223 407**		
		(8.4% of world production)		

Source: United States Geological Survey (USGS) 2011 Minerals Yearbook

Table 32
World Iron Ore Production in 2011

	Country	Production (thousand tonnes)	% of Total Production	Cumulative % of Production
1.	China	1 330	45.2	45.2
2.	Australia	488	16.6	61.8
3.	Brazil	373	12.7	74.5
4.	India	240	8.2	82.7
5.	Russia	100	3.4	86.1
6.	Ukraine	81	2.8	88.9
7.	South Africa	60	2.0	90.9
8.	United States	55	1.9	92.8
9.	Canada	34	1.2	94.0
10.	Iran	28	1,0	95.0
11.	Kazakhstan	25	0.9	95.9
12.	Sweden	25	0.9	96.8
13.	Venezuela	17	0.6	97.4
14.	Mexico	15	0.5	97.9
15.	Mauritania	12	0.4	98.3
16.	Others	59	2.0	100.3
	TOTAL	**2 940**		

Source: United States Geological Survey (USGS) 2011 Minerals Yearbook

Table 32

World Iron Ore Production in 2011

	Country	Production (million tonnes, gross weight)	% of Total Production	Cumulative % of Total Production
1.	China	1 330	45.2	45.2
2.	Australia	488	16.6	61.8
3.	Brazil	373	12.7	74.5
4.	India	240	8.2	82.7
5.	Russia	100	3.4	86.1
6.	Ukraine	81	2.8	88.9
7.	South Africa	60	2.0	90.9
8.	United States	55	1.9	92.8
9.	Canada	34	1.2	94.0
10.	Iran	28	1,0	95.0
11.	Kazakhstan	25	0.9	95.9
12.	Sweden	25	0.9	96.8
13.	Venezuela	17	0.6	97.4
14.	Mexico	15	0.5	97.9
15.	Mauritania	12	0.4	98.3
16.	Others	59	2.0	100.3
	TOTAL	**2 940**		

Source: United States Geological Survey (USGS) 2011 Minerals Yearbook

Table 33
European Iron Ore Production in 2011

	Country	Production (thousand tonnes, gross weight)	% of Total Production	Cumulative % of Total Production
1.	Russia	100 000	47.4	47.4
2.	Ukraine	81 000	38.4	85.8
3.	Sweden	25 000	11.8	97.6
4.	Austria	2 050	1.0	98.6
5.	Bosnia	1 850	0.9	99.5
6.	Norway	700	0.3	99.8
7.	Germany	400	0.2	100.0
8.	Portugal	14	0.0	
	TOTAL	**211 014**		
		(7.2% of world production)		

Source: United States Geological Survey (USGS) 2011 Minerals Yearbook

Table 34
World Lead Production in 2011

	Country	Production (thousand tonnes, gross weight)	% of Total Production	Cumulative % of Total Production
1.	China	2 350	50.0	50.0
2.	Australia	621	13.2	63.2
3.	United States	342	7.3	70.5
4.	Peru	230	4.9	75.4
5.	Mexico	220	4.7	80.1
6.	India	115	2.4	82.5
7.	Russia	105	2.2	84.7
8.	Bolivia	100	2.1	86.8
9.	Sweden	62	1.3	88.1
10.	Poland	60	1.3	89.4
11.	Canada	59	1.3	90.7
12.	South Africa	55	1.2	91.9
13.	Ireland	45	1.0	92.9
14.	Others	340	7.2	100.1
	TOTAL	**4 704**		

Source: United States Geological Survey (USGS) 2011 Minerals Yearbook

Table 34
World Lead Production in 2011

	Country	Production (thousand tonnes, lead content)	% of Total Production	Cumulative % of Total Production
1.	China	2 350	50.0	50.0
2.	Australia	621	13.2	63.2
3.	United States	342	7.3	70.5
4.	Peru	230	4.9	75.4
5.	Mexico	220	4.7	80.1
6.	India	115	2.4	82.5
7.	Russia	105	2.2	84.7
8.	Bolivia	100	2.1	86.8
9.	Sweden	62	1.3	88.1
10.	Poland	60	1.3	89.4
11.	Canada	59	1.3	90.7
12.	South Africa	55	1.2	91.9
13.	Ireland	45	1.0	92.9
14.	Others	340	7.2	100.1
	TOTAL	4 704		

Source: United States Geological Survey (USGS) 2011 Minerals Yearbook

Table 35
European Lead Production in 2011

	Country	Production (thousand tonnes, lead content)	% of Total Production	Cumulative % of Total Production
1.	Russia	105	30.2	30.2
2.	Sweden	62	17.9	48.1
3.	Poland	60	17.2	65.3
4.	Ireland	45	12.9	78.2
5.	Macedonia	40	11.5	89.7
6.	Greece	18	5.2	94.9
7.	Bulgaria	12	3.4	98.3
8.	Bosnia	3	0.9	99.2
9.	Serbia	2	0.6	99.8
10.	Italy	1	0.3	100.1
	TOTAL	**348**		
		(7.4% of World Production)		

Source: United States Geological Survey (USGS) 2011 Minerals Yearbook

Table 36
World Manganese Production in 2011

	Country	Production (thousand tonnes, metal content)	% of Total Production	Cumulative % of Total Production
1.	South Africa	3 400	20.7	20.7
2.	Australia	3 200	19.4	40.1
3.	China	2 800	17.0	57.1
4.	Gabon	1 860	11.3	68.4
5.	Brazil	1 210	7.4	75.8
6.	India	895	5.4	81.2
7.	Kazakhstan	390	2.4	83.6
8.	Ukraine	330	2.0	85.6
9.	Burma	234	1.4	87.0
10.	Malaysia	225	1.4	88.4
11.	Mexico	171	1.0	89.4
12.	Others	1 740	10.6	100.0
	TOTAL	**16 455**		

Source: United States Geological Survey (USGS) 2011 Minerals Yearbook

Table 37
European Manganese Production

	Country	Production (thousand tonnes, metal content)	% of Total Production	Cumulative % of Total Production
1.	Ukraine	330	78.9	78.9
2.	Bulgaria	42	10.0	88.9
3.	Russia	30	7.2	96.1
4.	Hungary	16	3.8	99.9
	TOTAL	**418**		
		(2.5% of world production)		

Source: United States Geological Survey (USGS) 2011 Minerals Yearbook.

Table 38
World Mercury Production in 2011

	Country	Production (tonnes, metal content)	% of Total Production	Cumulative % of Total Production
1.	China	1 350	74.5	74.5
2.	Kyrgyzstan	250	13.8	88.3
3.	Chile	52	2.9	91.2
4.	Russia	50	2.8	94.0
5.	Peru	40	2.2	96.2
6.	Tajikistan	30	1.7	97.9
7.	Mexico	21	1.2	99.1
8.	Others	20	1.1	100.2
	TOTAL	**1 813**		

Source: United States Geological Survey (USGS)

Table 39
World Nickel Production in 2011

	Country	Production (tonnes, metal content)	% of Total Production	Cumulative % of Total Production
1.	Indonesia	290 000	15.0	15.0
2.	Philippines	270 000	13.9	28.9
3.	Russia	267 000	13.8	42.7
4.	Canada	220 000	11.3	54.0
5.	Australia	215 000	11.1	65.1
6.	New Caledonia	131 000	6.8	71.9
7.	Brazil	109 000	5.6	77.5
8.	China	89 000	4.6	82.1
9.	Colombia	76 000	3.9	86.0
10.	Cuba	71 000	3.7	89.7
11.	South Africa	44 000	2.3	92.0
12.	Botswana	26 000	1.3	93.3
13.	Dominican Republic	21 700	1.1	94.4
14.	Madagascar	5 900	0.3	94.7
15.	Others	103 000	5.3	100.0
	TOTAL	**1 938 600**		

Source: United States Geological Survey (USGS)

Table 40
European Nickel Production in 2011

	Country	Production (tonnes, metal content)	% of Total Production	Cumulative % of Total Production
1.	Russia	267 000	86.0	86.0
2.	Finland	21 710	7.0	93.0
3.	Greece	18 300	5.9	98.9
4.	Albania	3 500	1.1	100.0
	TOTAL	**310 510**		
	(16% of world production)			

Source: United States Geological Survey (USGS)

Table 41
World Platinum Production in 2011

	Country	Production (kilograms)	% of Total Production	Cumulative % of Total Production
1.	South Africa	145 000	74.3	74.3
2.	Russia	25 000	12.8	87.1
3.	Zimbabwe	10 600	5.4	92.5
4.	Canada	7 000	3.6	96.1
5.	United States	3 700	1.9	98.0
6.	Colombia	1 230	0.6	98.6
7.	Others	2 500	1.3	99.9
	TOTAL	**195 030**		

Source: United States Geological Survey (USGS)

Table 42
European Production of Platinum

	Country	Production (kilograms)	% of Total Production	Cumulative % of Total Production
1.	Russia	25 000	98.3	98.3
2.	Finland	400	1.6	99.9
3.	Poland	25	0.1	100.0
	TOTAL	**25 425**		
	(13% of World Production)			

Source: United States Geological Survey (USGS)

Table 43
World Silver Production in 2011

	Country	Production (kilograms)	% of Total Production	Cumulative % of Total Production
1.	Mexico	4 150	17.8	17.8
2.	China	3 700	15.9	33.7
3.	Peru	3 410	14.6	48.3
4.	Australia	1 730	7.4	55.4
5.	Russia	1 350	5.8	61.5
6.	Chile	1 290	5.5	67.0
7.	Bolivia	1 210	5.2	72.2
8.	Poland	1 170	5.0	77.2
9.	United States	1 120	4.8	82.0
10.	Canada	572	2.5	84.5
11.	Others	3 600	15.4	99.9
	TOTAL	23 302		

Source: United States Geological Survey (USGS)

Table 44
Table 44
European Silver Production

	Country	Production (kilograms)	% of Total Production	Cumulative % of Total Production
1.	Russia	1 350	45.3	45.3
2.	Poland	1 170	39.2	84.5
3.	Sweden	270	9.1	93.6
4.	Finland	70	2.3	95.9
5.	Bulgaria	55	1.8	97.7
6.	Greece	30	1.0	98.7
7.	Portugal	24	0.8	99.5
8.	Others	13	0.4	99.9
	TOTAL	**2 982**		
	(12.8% of World Production)			

Source: United States Geological Survey (USGS)

Table 45

World Tin Production in 2011

	Country	Production (kilograms)	% of Total Production	Cumulative % of Total Production
1.	China	120 000	49.1	49.1
2.	Indonesia	42 000	17.2	66.3
3.	Peru	28 900	11.8	78.1
4.	Bolivia	20 300	8.3	86.4
5.	Brazil	11 000	4.5	90.9
6.	Australia	6 500	2.7	93.6
7.	Vietnam	5 400	2.2	95.8
8.	Malaysia	3 350	1.4	97.2
9.	DRC	2 900	1.2	98.4
10.	Rwanda	1 400	0.6	99.0
11.	Thailand	200	0.1	99.1
12.	Russia	160	0.1	99.2
13.	Others	2 000	0.8	100.0
	TOTAL	**244 110**		

Source: United States Geological Survey (USGS)

Table 46

European Tin Production in 2011

	Country	Production (kilograms)	% of Total Production	Cumulative % of Total Production
1.	Russia	160	84.2	84.2
2.	Portugal	30	15.8	100.0
	TOTAL	**190**		
		(0.1% of world production)		

Source: United States Geological Survey (USGS)

Table 47
World Zinc Production

	Country	Production (thousand tonnes)	% of Total Production	Cumulative % of Total Production
1.	China	4 310	33.7	33.7
2.	Australia	1 520	11.9	45.6
3.	Peru	1 260	9.8	55.4
4.	United States	769	6.0	61.4
5.	India	710	5.5	66.9
6.	Mexico	632	4.9	71.8
7.	Canada	612	4.8	76.6
8.	Kazakhstan	495	3.9	80.5
9.	Bolivia	427	3.3	83.8
10.	Ireland	340	2.7	86.5
11.	Others	1 730	13.5	100.0
	TOTAL	**12 805**		

Source: United States Geological Survey (USGS)

Table 48
European Zinc Production

	Country	Production (thousand tonnes)	% of Total Production	Cumulative % of Total Production
1.	Ireland	340	32.9	32.9
2.	Russia	280	27.0	59.9
3.	Sweden	194	18.7	78.6
4.	Poland	68	6.6	85.2
5.	Finland	64	6.2	91.4
6.	Macedonia	36	3.5	94.9
7.	Spain	33	3.2	98.1
8.	Bulgaria	8	0.8	98.9
9.	Bosnia	6	0.6	99.5
10.	Portugal	4	0.4	99.9
11.	Serbia	2	0.2	100.1
	TOTAL	**1 035**		
		(8.1% of world production)		

Source: United States Geological Survey (USGS)